How to Draw Planes (This How to Draw Planes Book Contains Tips on How to Draw 40 Different Airplanes)

Includes instructions on how to draw a jet plane, a realistic plane, and vintage planes

James Manning

HOW TO DRAW PLANES

Introduction for Parents

Drawing is an essential part of a child's development, stimulating parts of the brain that are responsible for creative thinking and imagination. From a young age, we are all creatively encouraged to draw, whether it be at home or pre-school. Drawing is often encouraged to improve our fine motor skills and hand-eye co-ordination; this co-ordination is vital for future academic success and for improving our penmanship/handwriting skills.

From toddler's 'scribbles' to more refined 'matchstick men' and recognisable shapes, you may find that as your child grows they will want to tackle a more complex way of drawing (perhaps it's an image they have seen in a book) but as they begin to put pencil to paper they may have no idea where to start, causing frustration and annoyance.

With the help of our 'How to Draw' book series, this frustration will disappear as we guide your child step by step, line by line, to create their very own masterpiece!

Each illustration is deconstructed and simplified into lines and shapes which will not overwhelm your child. As we guide them to form each simple line and shape together on the paper, the image gradually becomes more detailed, textured and visually appealing. Practice will always make perfect, so encouraging your child to repeat the initial steps will incite a sense of self assurance that they are able to improve their skill line by line.

If Your Child Struggles With This Book

The rate of cognitive development varies from child to child and, as such, where one child may be ready for this book another will not. If you feel that your child is not ready for this book at the moment, take it away and bring it back to them in six to twelve months.

If your child is not ready to draw step-by-step, he or she may prefer to work using grids. Grid drawing involves copying information from one grid to another using coordinates. The type of copying required in grid drawing is very useful for the brain as, in particular, it exercises working memory. Working memory involves holding onto information temporarily and then using that temporarily held information at the same time. Working memory is an important process required in maintaining attention and exercising it will be beneficial for a range of activities, including in class at school.

Dr James Manning
Consultant Clinical Psychologist

HOW TO DRAW PLANES

Here are all of the drawings in this book. I guess it must seem like there is a lot of them when they are looked at all at once!

Luckily, I am not going to ask you to draw them all straight away. The best way to learn to draw is one step at a time. Each drawing in this book may require between 50 and 200 strokes of your pencil, but all you will need to think about is drawing one stroke at a time.

As you use your pencil, stroke by stroke, working your way through this book, you will eventually be able to create all of the drawings!

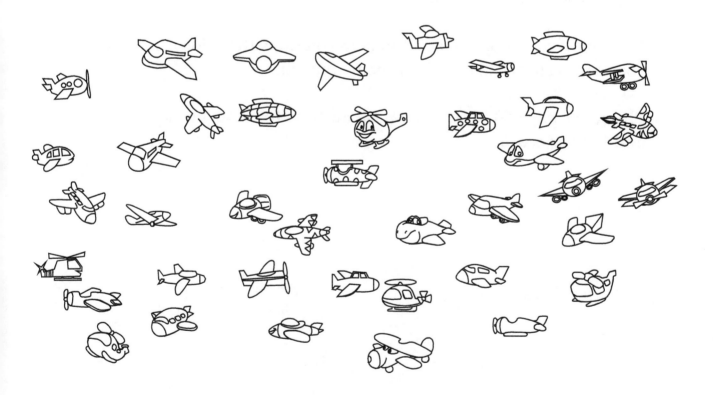

Drawing Step-by-Step

In this book I will show you how to create 40 different drawings step by step. Each step will build on the previous one until eventually you have 40 complete drawings.

At first, you find my step-by-step approach too complicated or difficult please leave it to one side and come back to it later. Instead, you may want to use an alternative grid with numbers and letters on it first. By following the coordinates and matching them up with the coordinates on a blank grid you can redraw the pictures this way instead.

I have put details below about where you can download these basic grids for free on the internet.

https://www.lipdf.com/product/grids/

You can of course ask an adult to help you draw the grids instead, or you may even feel able to draw them yourself.

Please see page 40 for the webpage address for your bonus books and the password.

1. The first stroke of your pencil can often be the most daunting but give it a go and see where the drawing takes you!

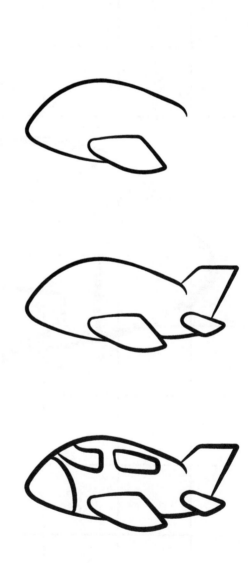

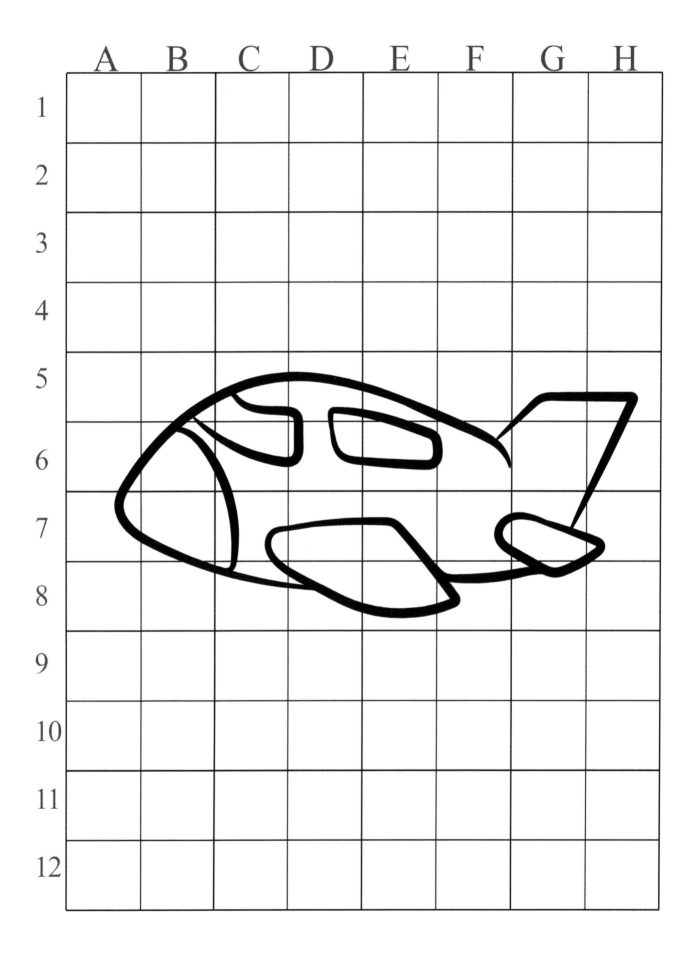

2. Have confidence with
your first pencil stroke,
don't overthink the
positioning too much!

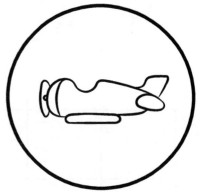

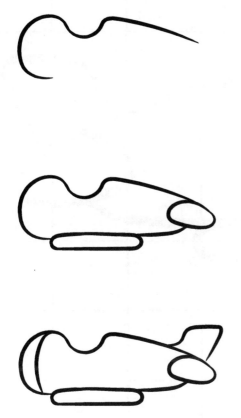

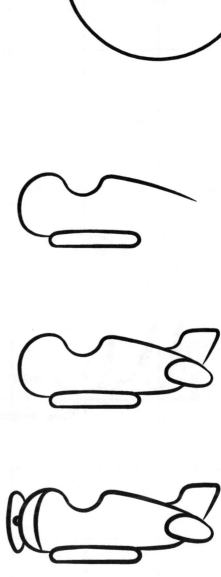

	A	B	C	D	E	F	G	H
1								
2								
3								
4								
5								
6								
7								
8								
9								
10								
11								
12								

3. Copying the lines exactly as they are shown in the book isn't a necessity, use the grids as a guide and source of inspiration for your own drawing.

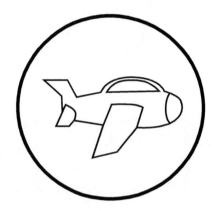

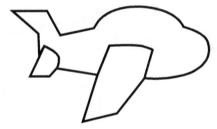

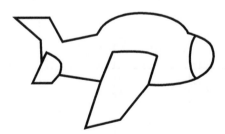

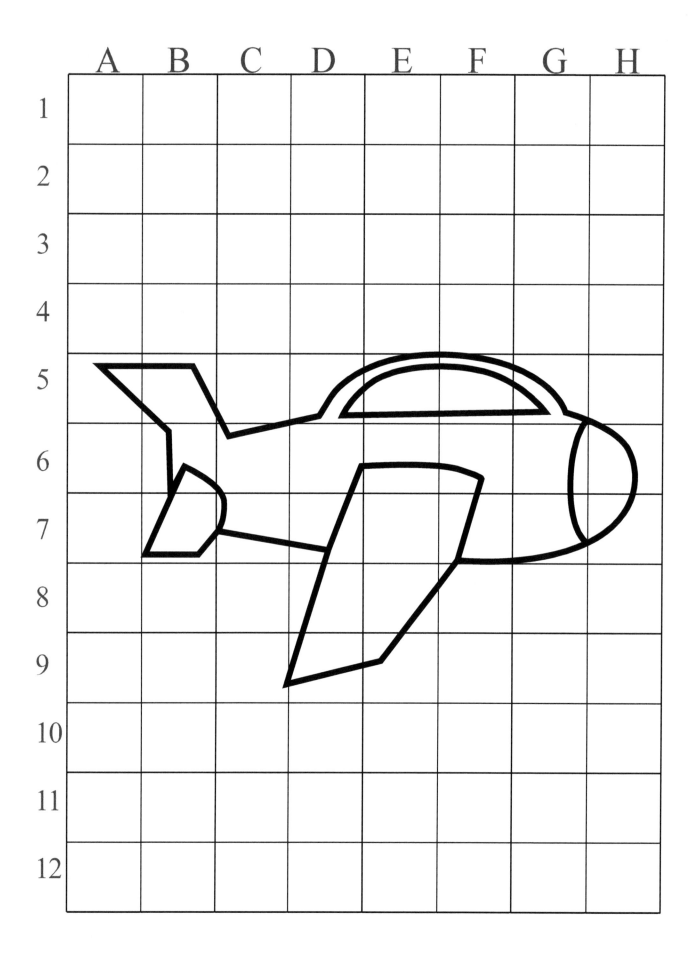

4. Don't get frustrated if you can't copy the lines exactly, just use them to point you in the right direction.

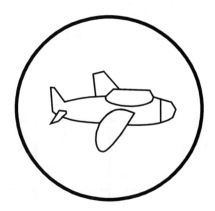

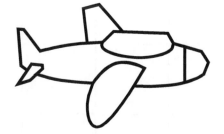

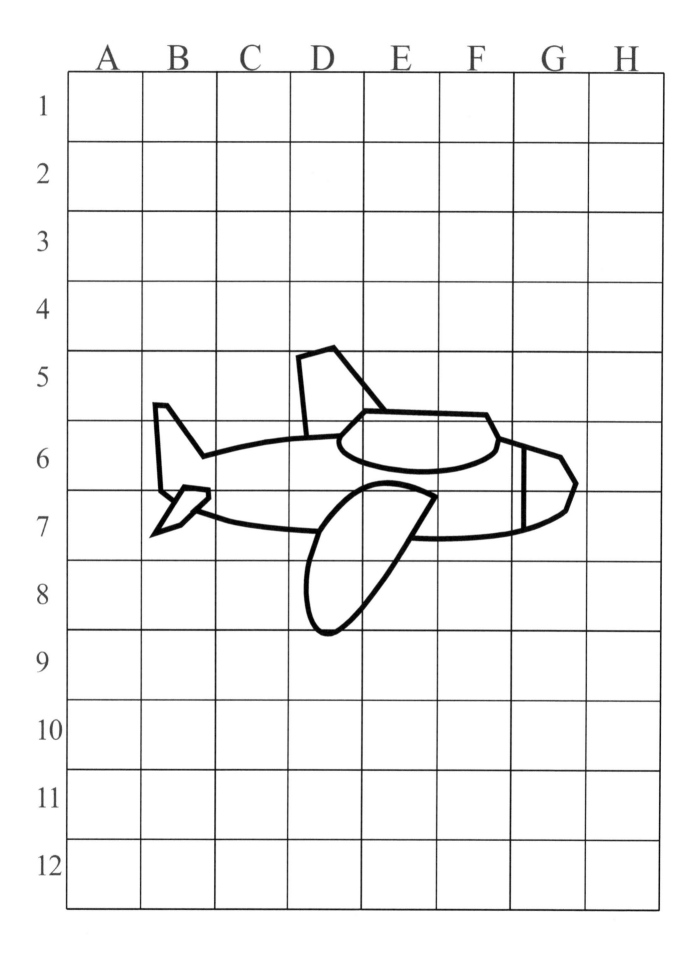

5. If you find you are getting frustrated with your drawing, take a break and come back to it later.

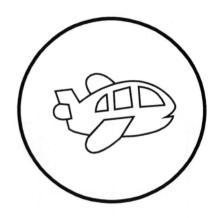

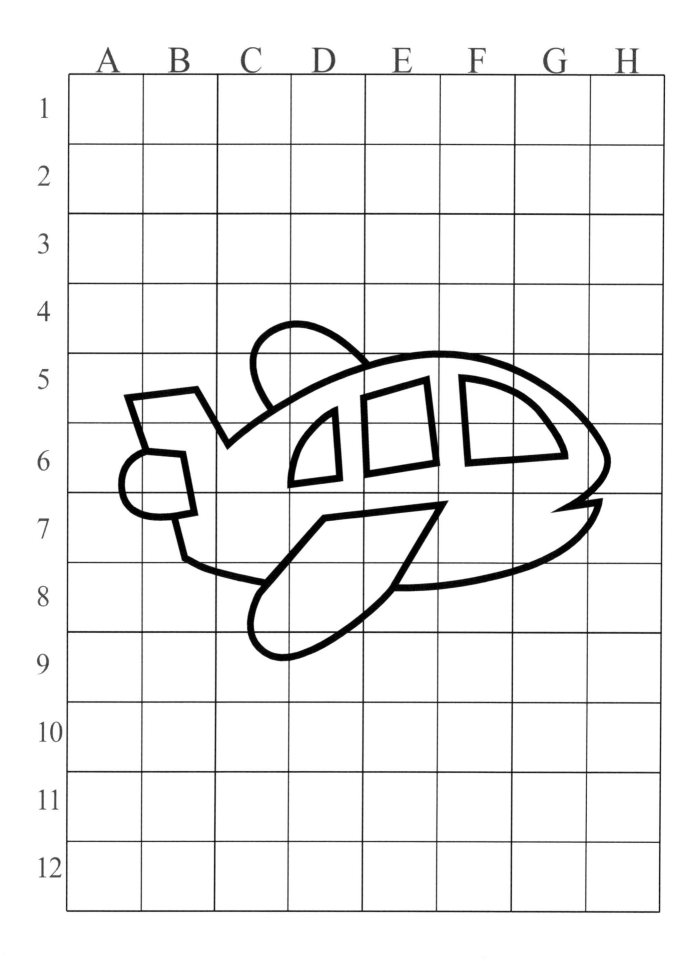

6. Take your time and keep practicing, everybody learns at different paces.

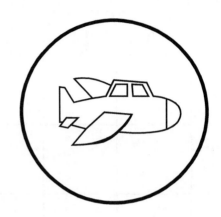

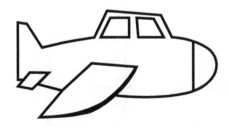

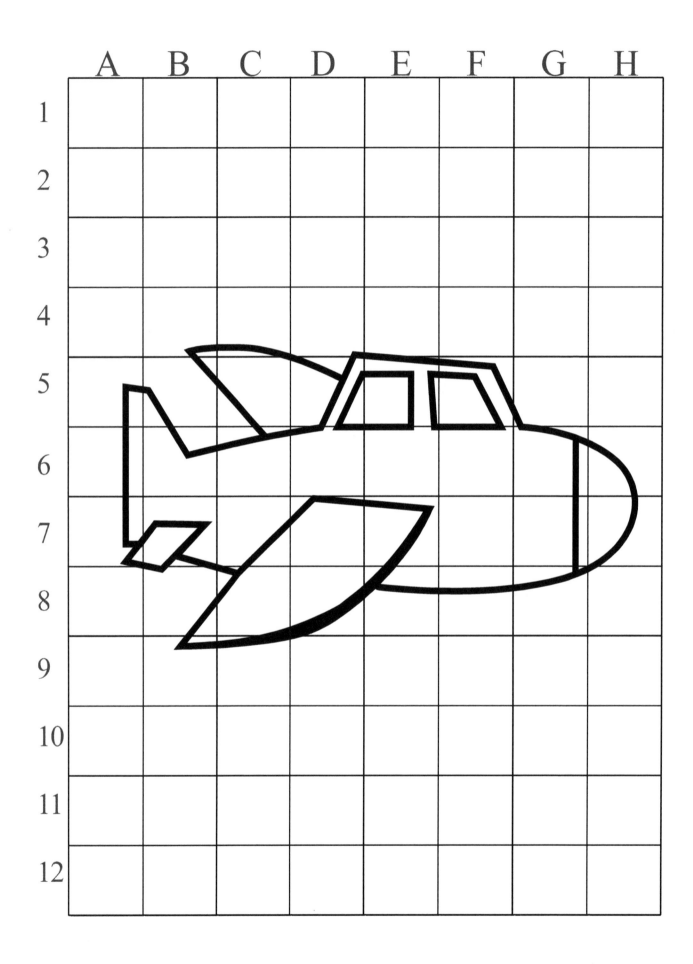

7. Don't worry if you are spending more time drawing a picture, it's more important to take your time when producing high quality work.

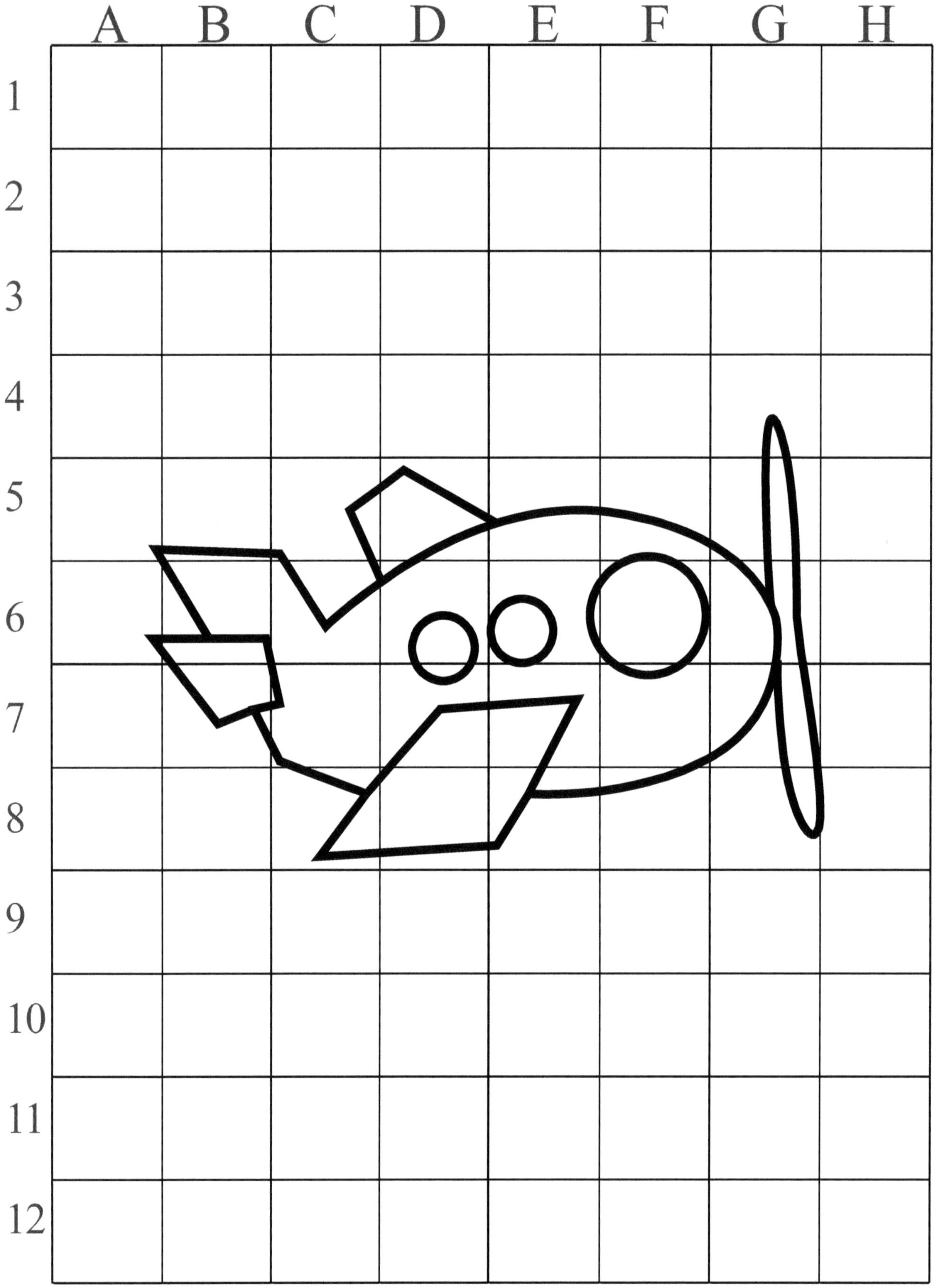
A B C D E F G H
1
2
3
4
5
6
7
8
9
10
11
12

8. Don't forget the grid is there to help you. Use it to help keep your drawing in proportion.

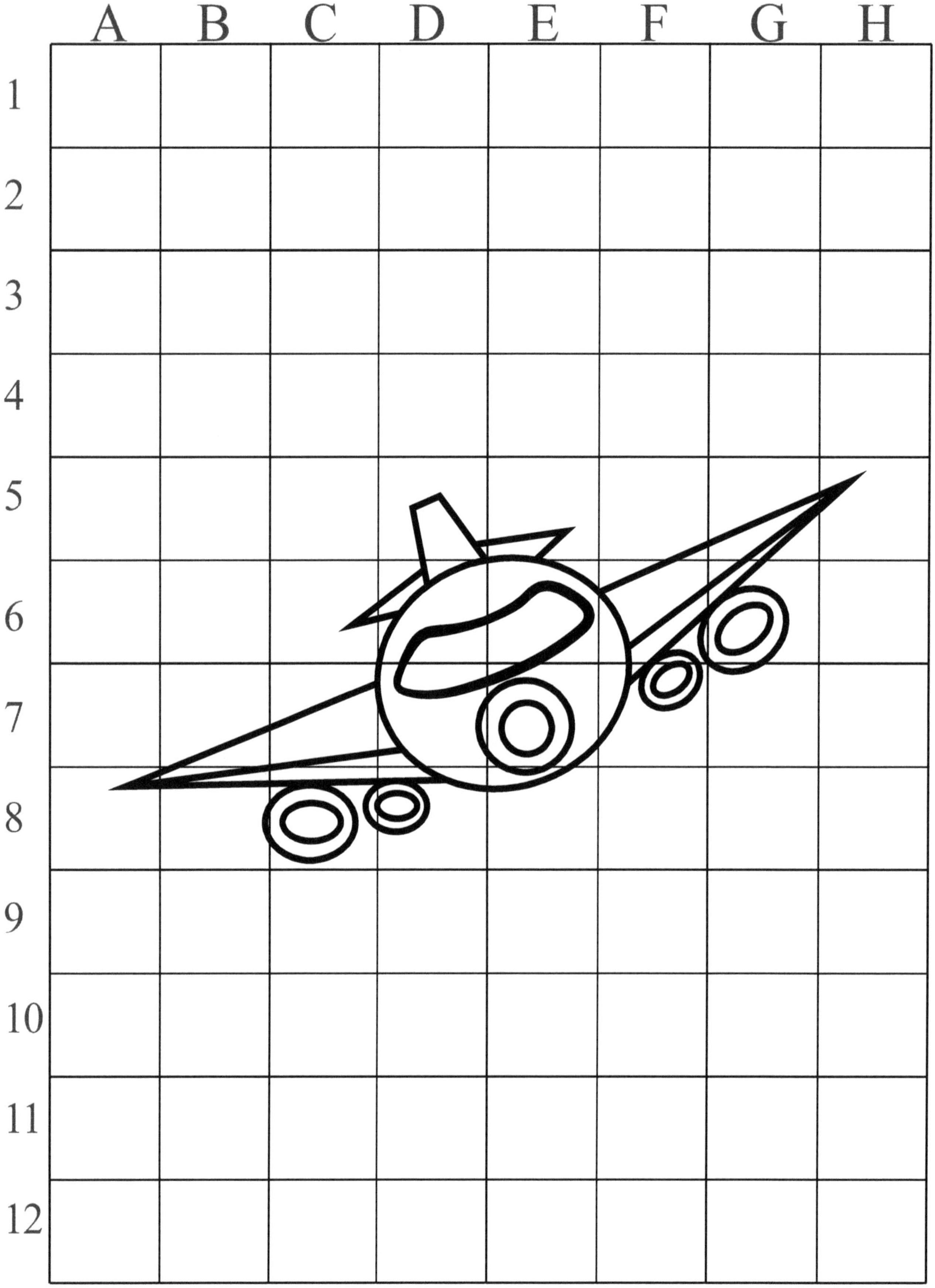
A
B
C
D
E
F
G
H
1
2
3
4
5
6
7
8
9
10
11
12

9. Focus on the larger
shapes first, then add in
the finer details.

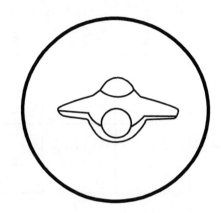

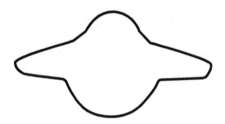

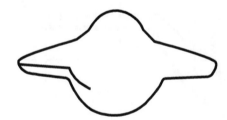

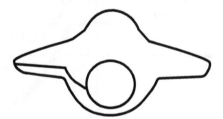

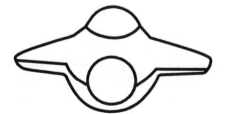

	A	B	C	D	E	F	G	H
1								
2								
3								
4								
5								
6								
7								
8								
9								
10								
11								
12								

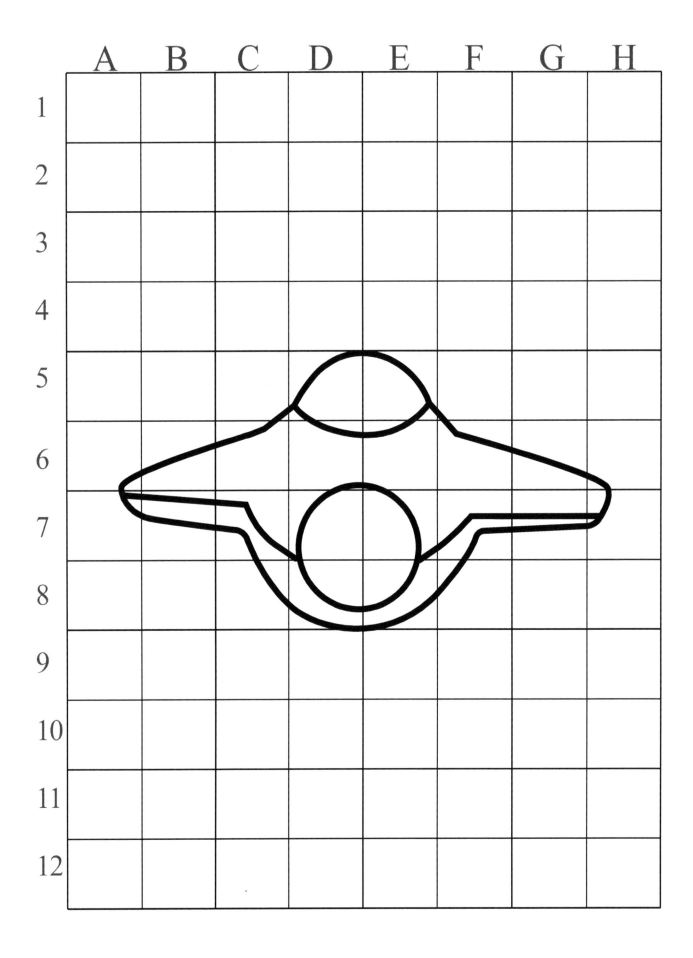

10. Focus on the larger shapes first, then add in the finer details.

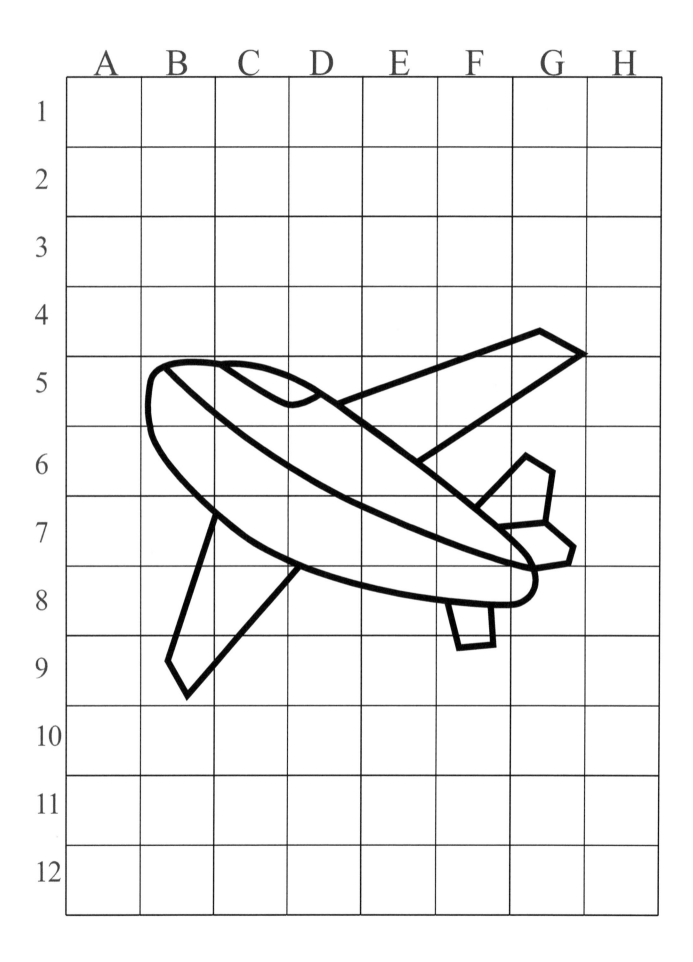

11. Have a go at colouring in your drawing once its finished!

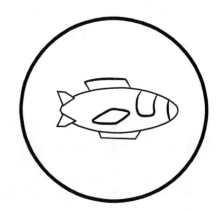

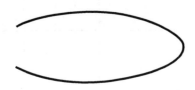

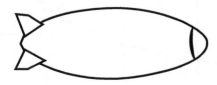

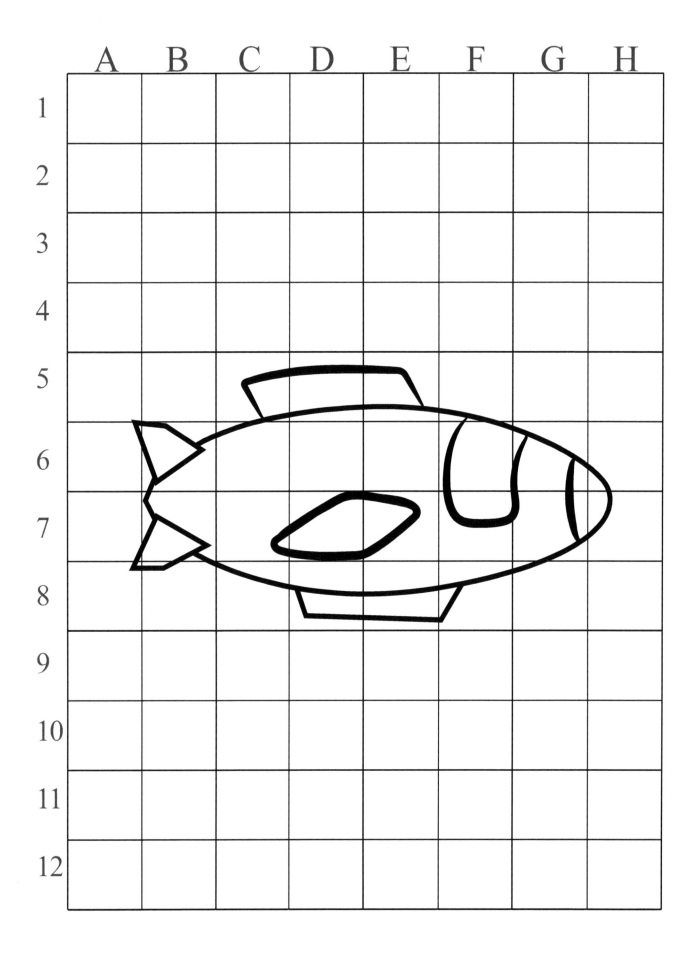

12. If you're using the
grid, take the drawing one
box at a time

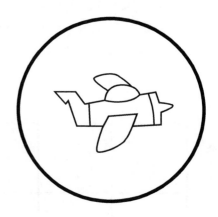

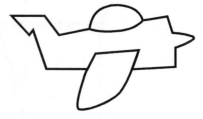

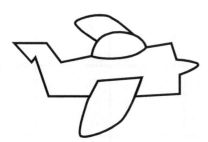

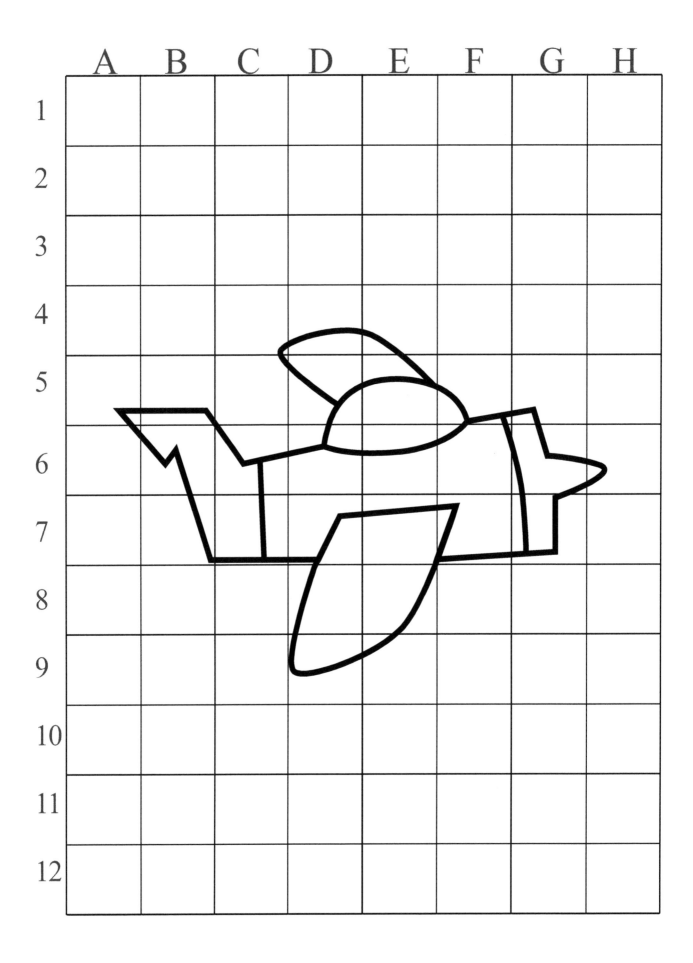

13. Keep positive when drawing. Don't tell yourself you "can't do it", but instead say "I can do this."

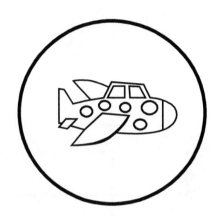

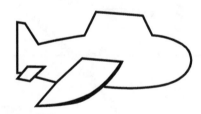

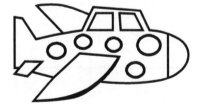

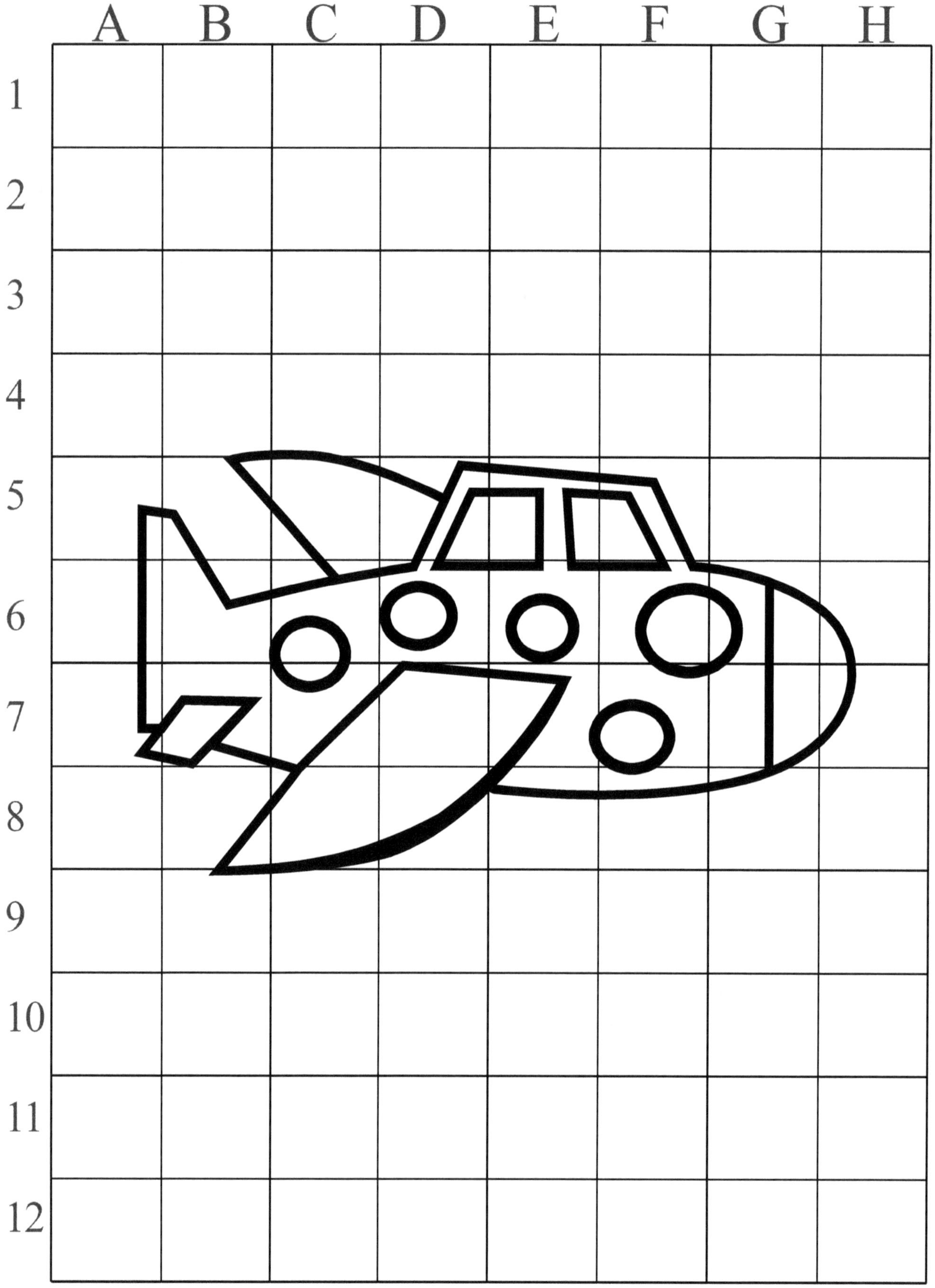
A B C D E F G H
1
2
3
4
5
6
7
8
9
10
11
12

14. Add in extra features to make you drawing unique and personal to you.

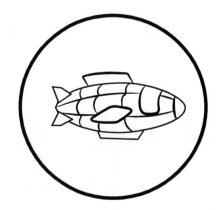

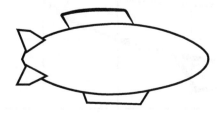

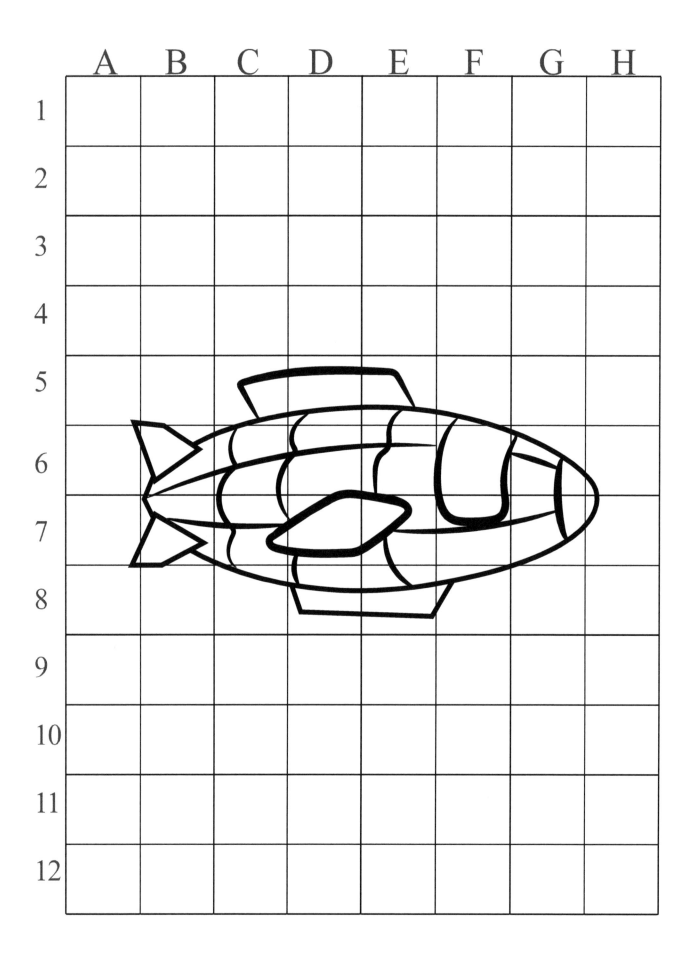

15. Once you have practiced using grids, in the future you may be able to draw the character from memory alone.

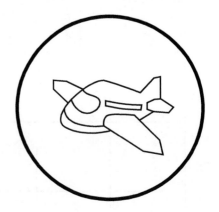

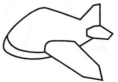

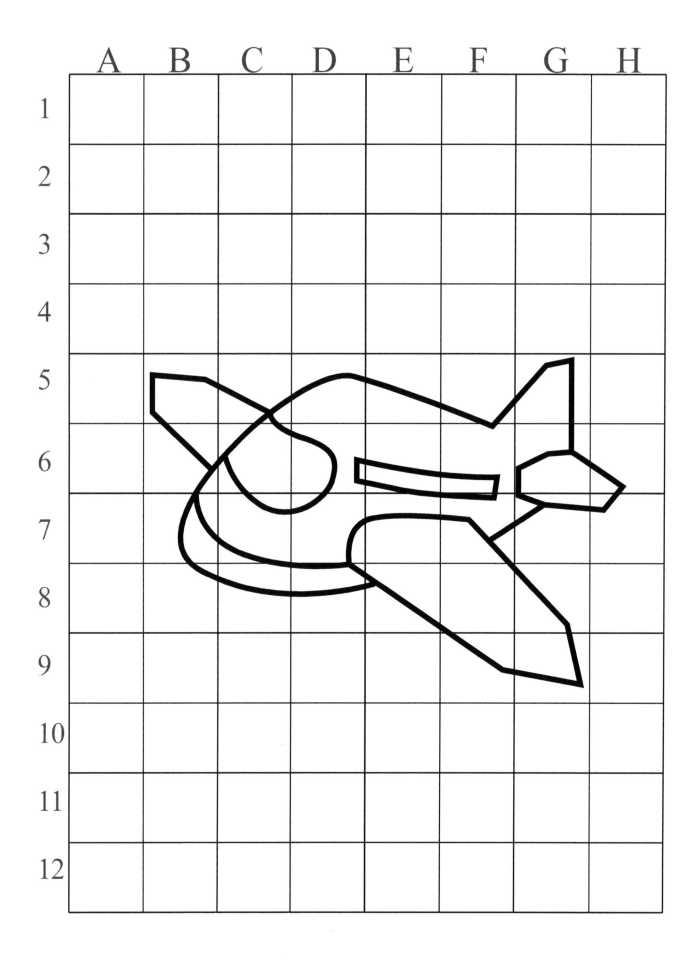

16. It's unlikely you will get everything right the first time. Draw in pencil so you can erase any mistakes.

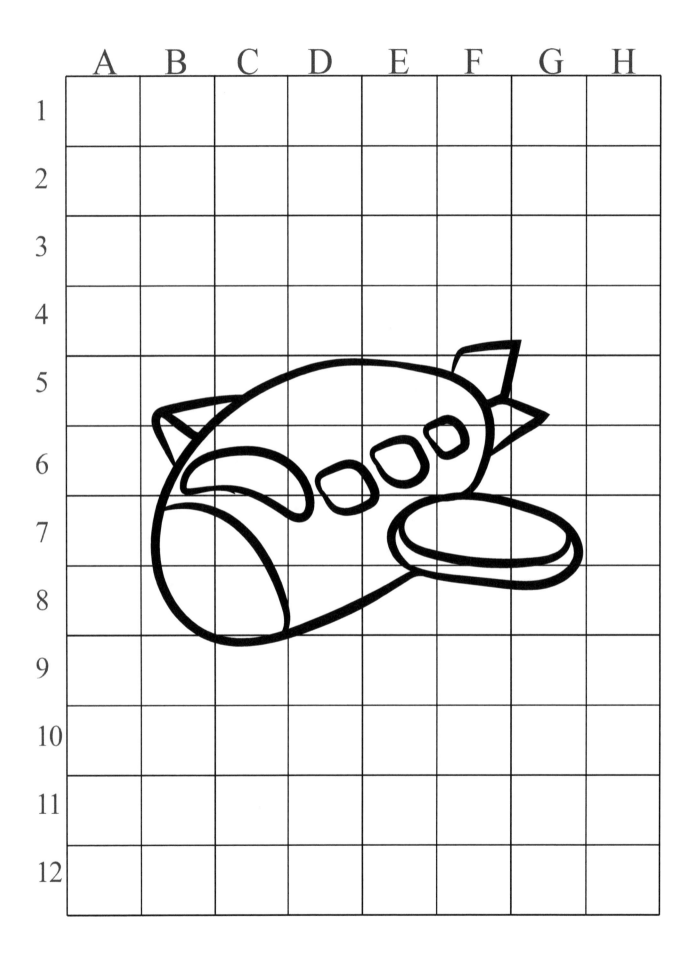

17. Why not experiment with how you hold your pencil? How you hold a pen for handwriting may not be comfortable for drawing.

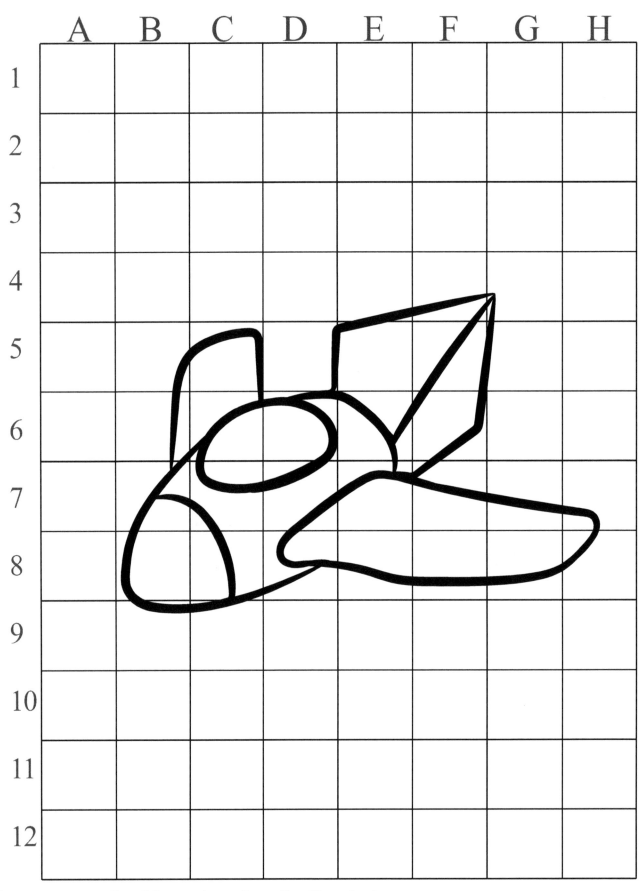

18. Artists never stop
learning, so never doubt
your talent.

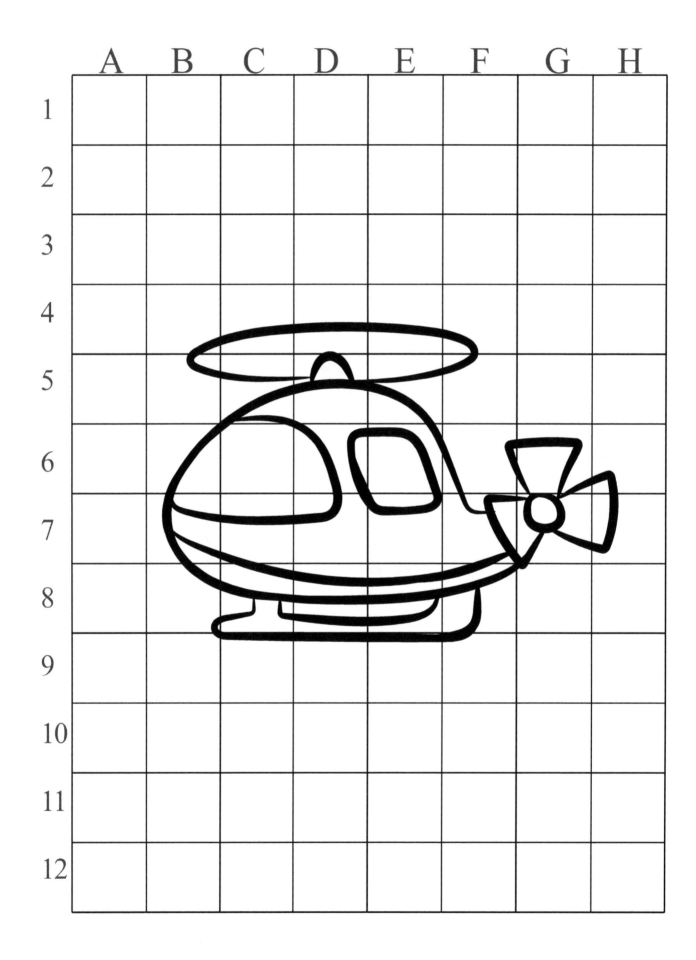

19. Patience is key. If you are getting irritated with your work, leave it for now and come back to it later.

	A	B	C	D	E	F	G	H
1								
2								
3								
4								
5								
6								
7								
8								
9								
10								
11								
12								

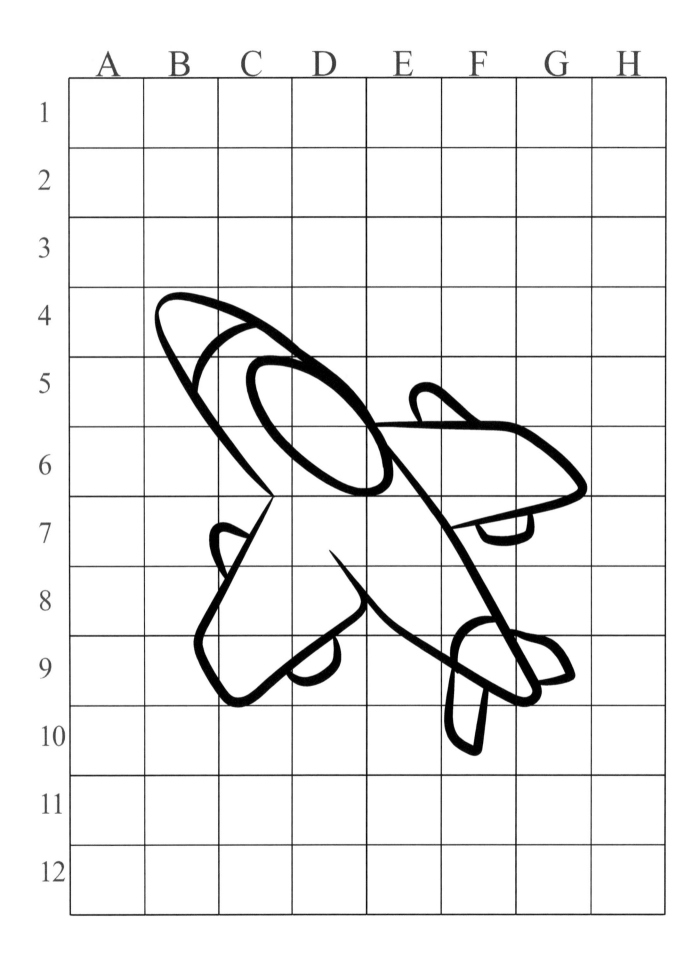

20. You could have a go at very roughly sketching out the shapes, then going over the lines in pen. Once finished, erase out the rough lines.

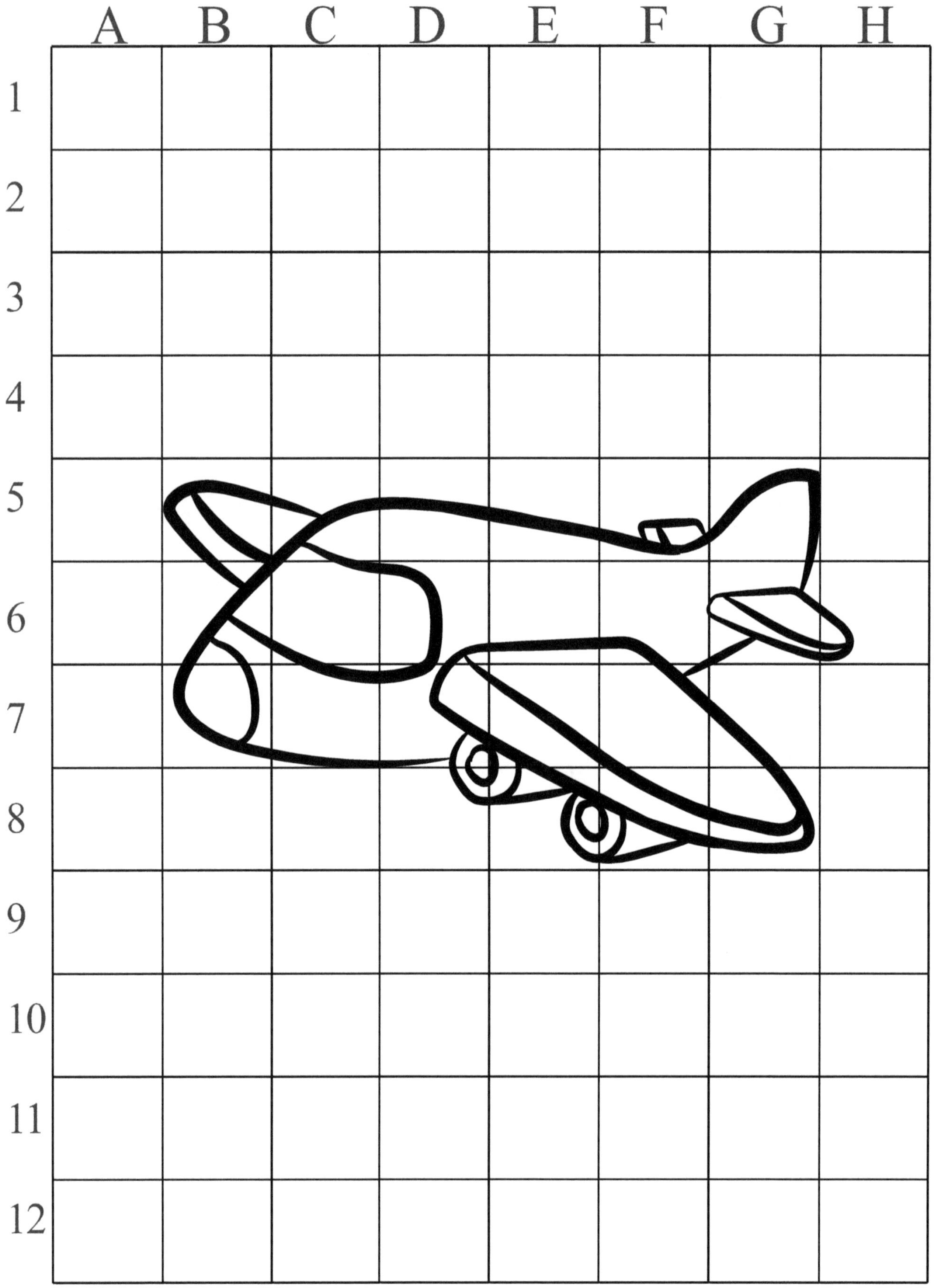
A
B
C
D
E
F
G
H
1
2
3
4
5
6
7
8
9
10
11
12

21. Improvement is all about recognising your mistakes, and trying not to make them a second time.

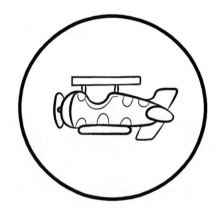

 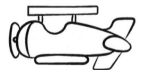 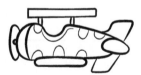

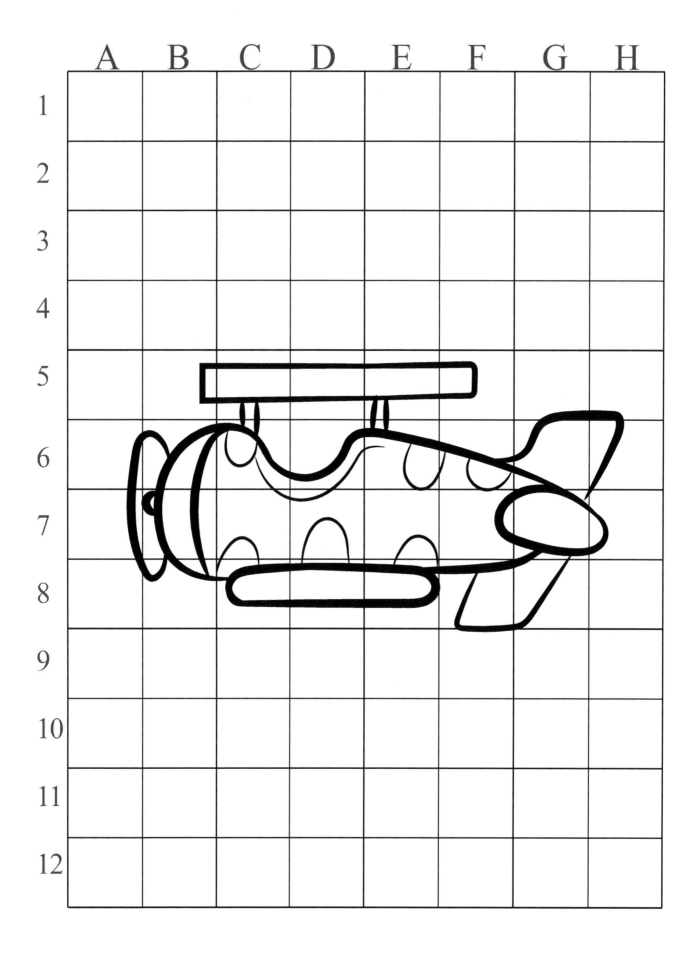

22. Drawing is all trial and error. How do you know how good or bad something looks without even trying to draw it?

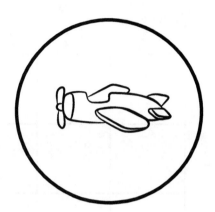

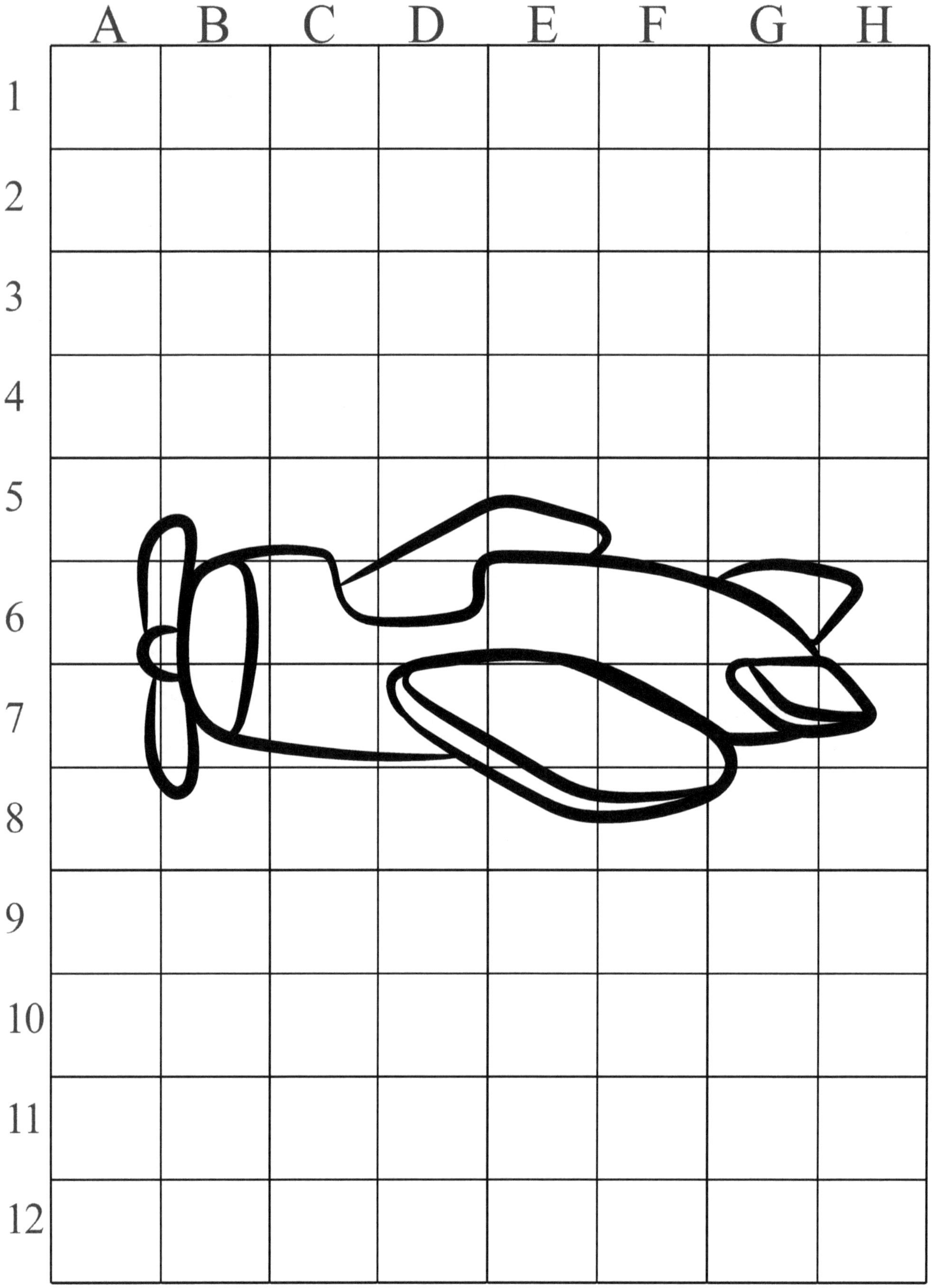
A B C D E F G H
1
2
3
4
5
6
7
8
9
10
11
12

23. If you struggle with this particular drawing, stop where you are and try another page in this book. You can always come back to this page later.

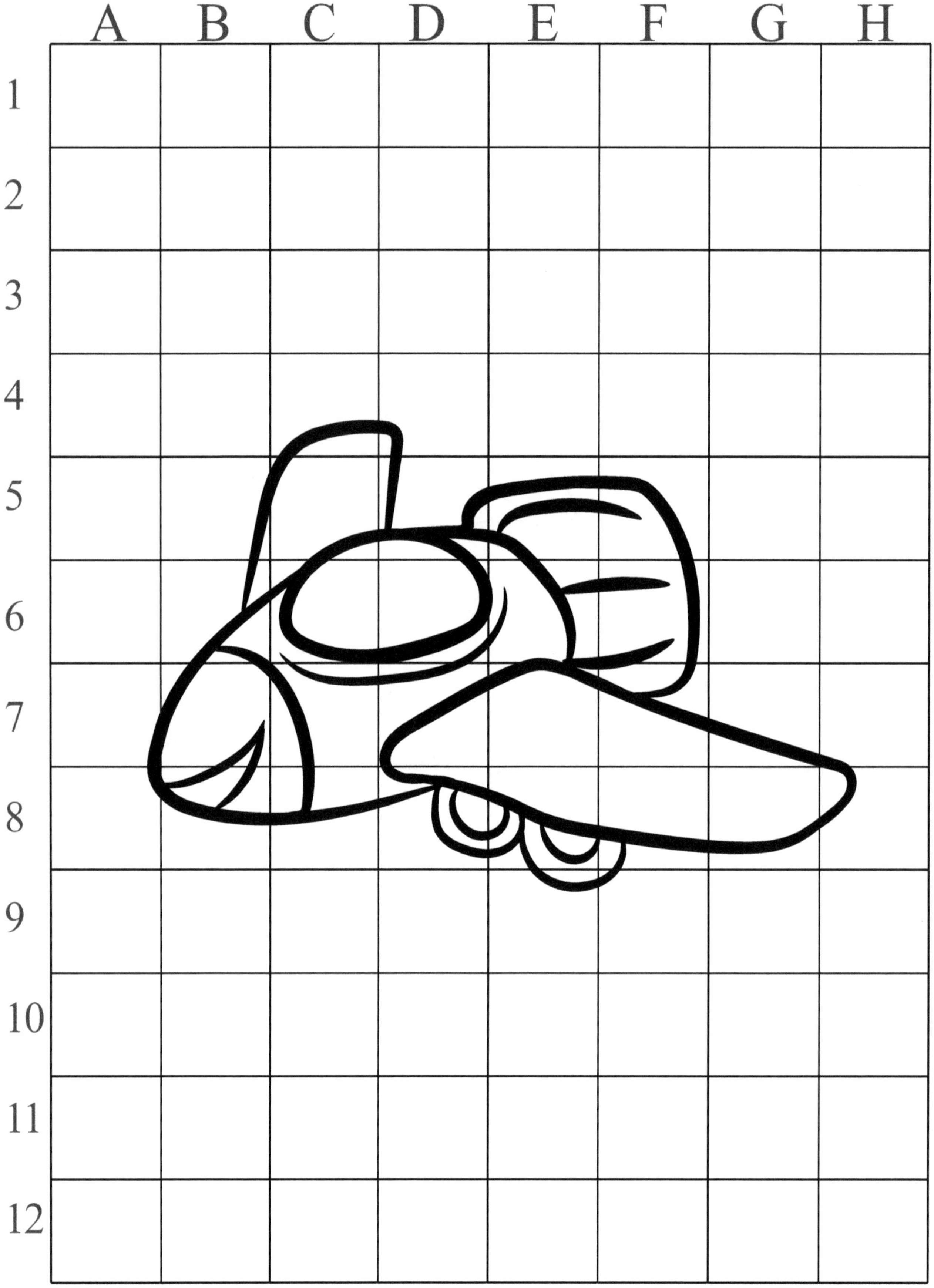
A B C D E F G H
1
2
3
4
5
6
7
8
9
10
11
12

24. Never doubt your potential, you are in control of your own progress.

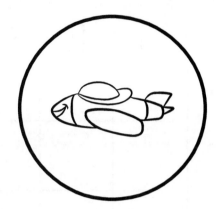

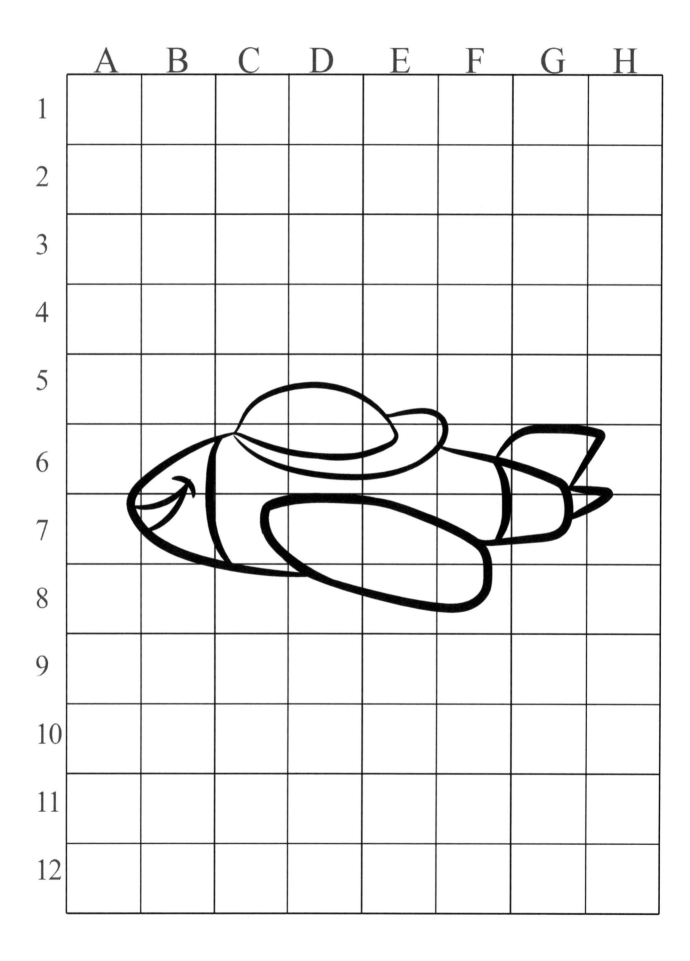

25. Drawing a little everyday will help your drawing improve, stick with it!

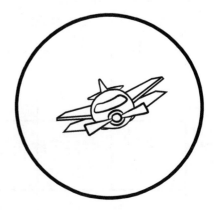

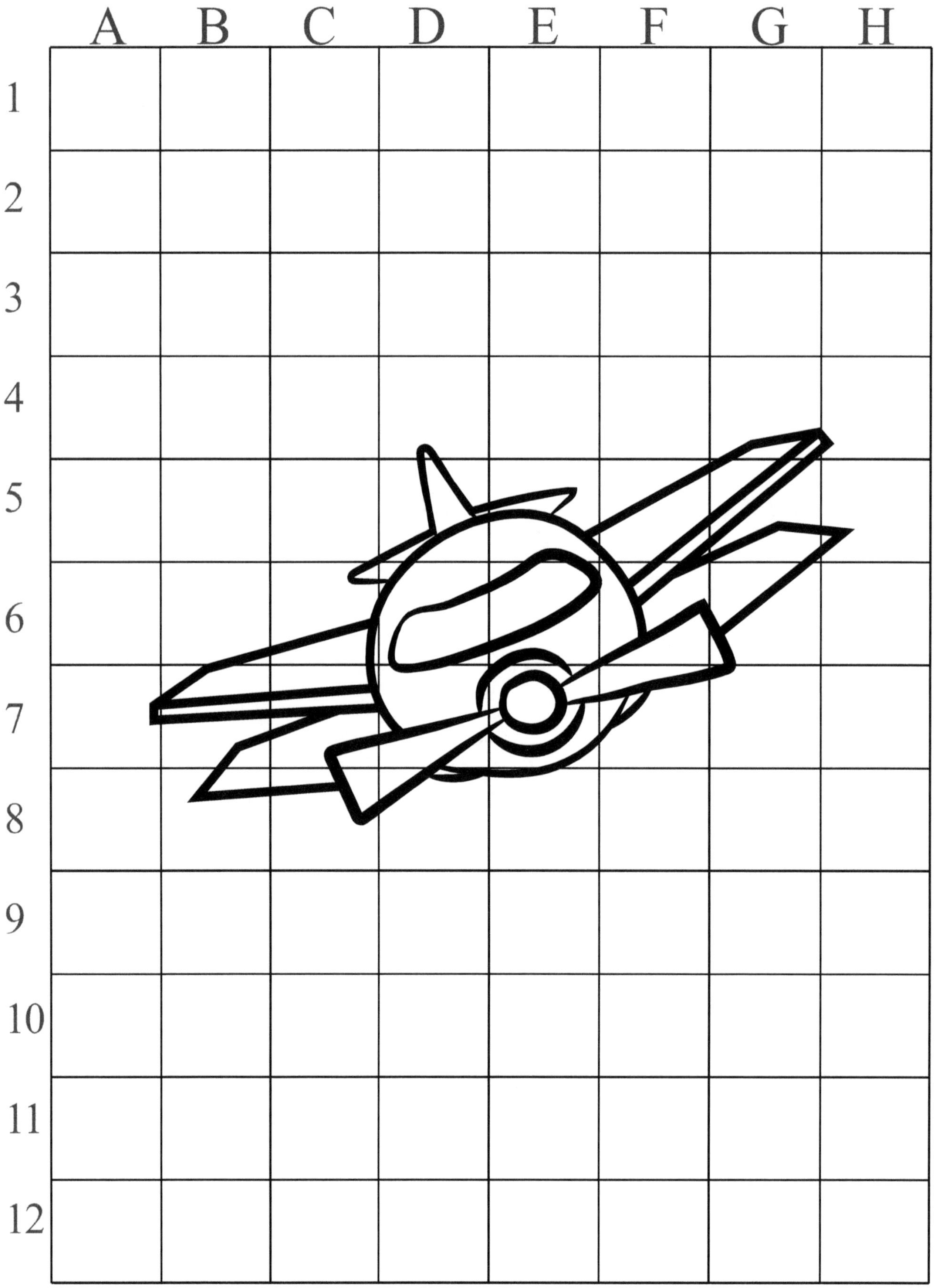
A
B
C
D
E
F
G
H
1
2
3
4
5
6
7
8
9
10
11
12

26. If you want to, you could practice different types of pencil strokes on a scrap piece of paper. What happens when you press hard with the pencil? What happens when you use the edge of the pencil rather than the point?

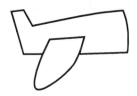

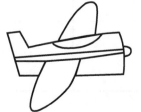

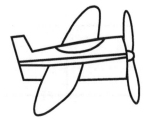

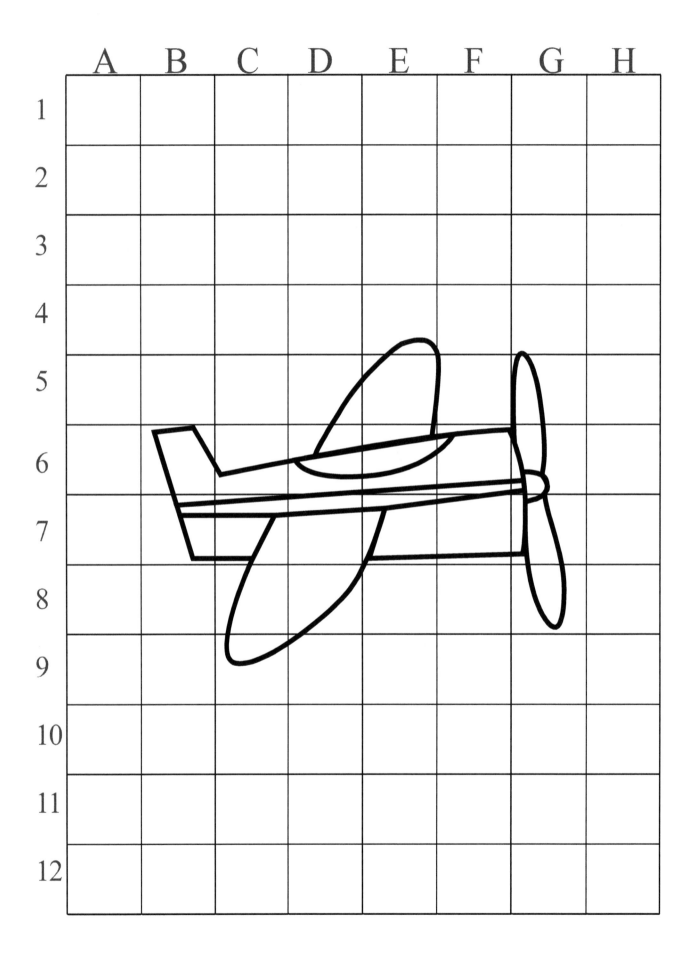

27. Always keep your hand relaxed, you will be surprised to see how your drawing flows on the paper when you aren't pressing too hard with the pencil.

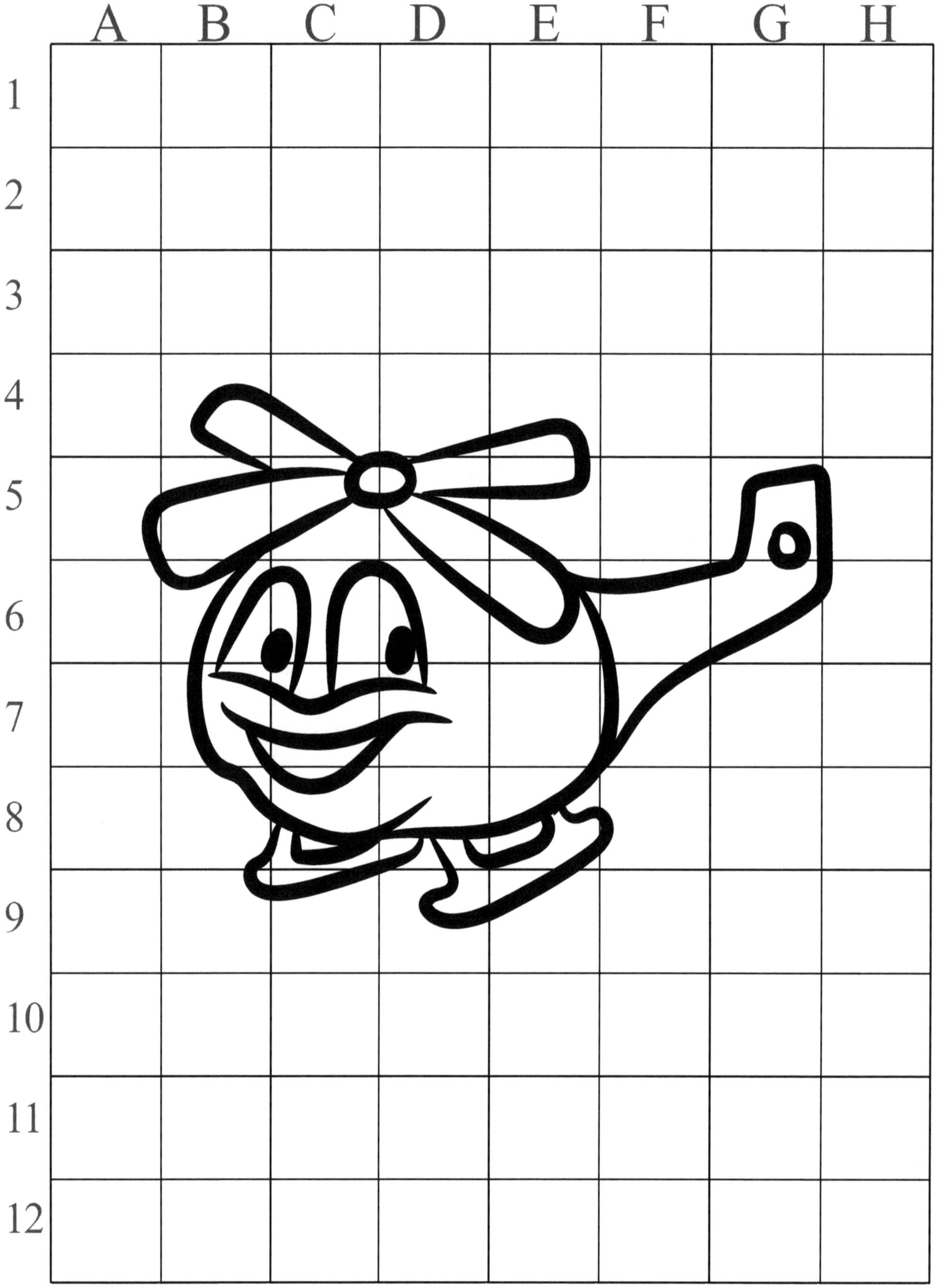
A
B
C
D
E
F
G
H
1
2
3
4
5
6
7
8
9
10
11
12

28. Try out a "warm up" exercise before starting your drawing. Have a go a straight, curved and zig zag lines on a scrap piece of paper.

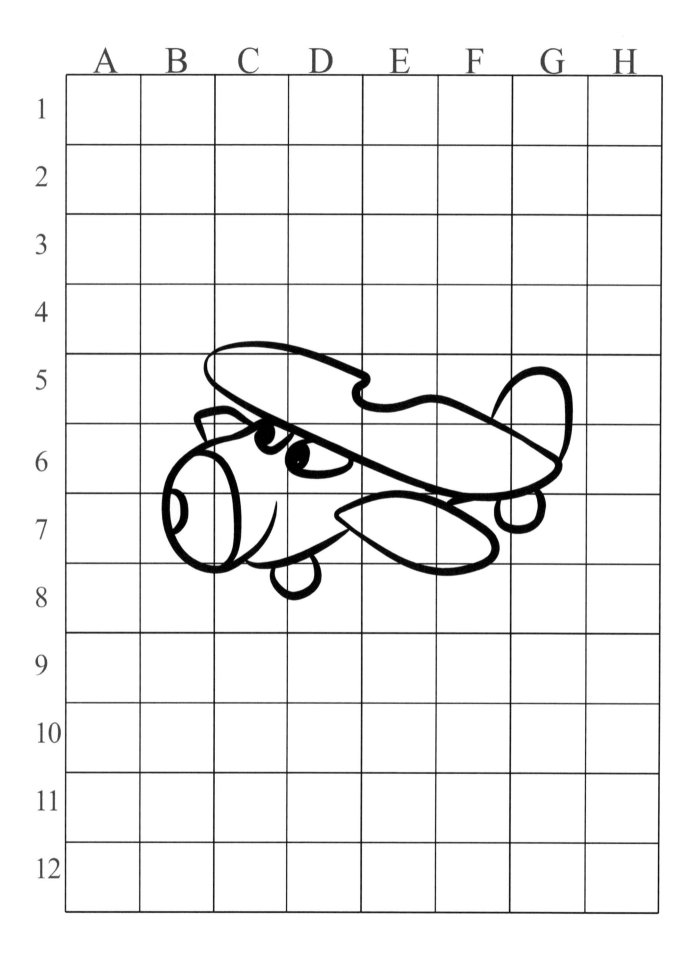

29. Try out doodling on a scrap piece of paper before starting this drawing, it will help with your concentration and creativity!

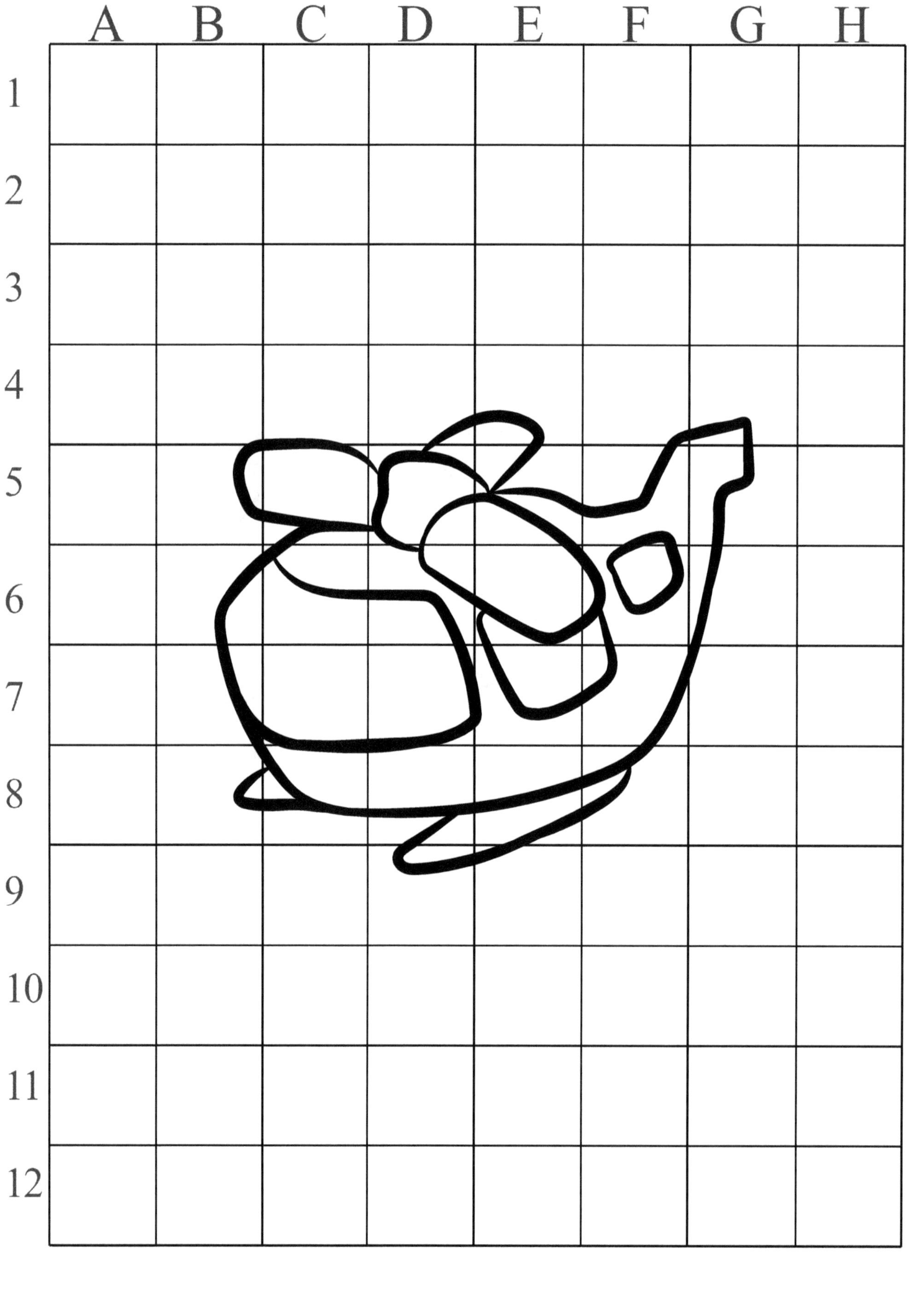
A B C D E F G H
1 2 3 4 5 6 7 8 9 10 11 12

30. If you are struggling to draw a long line, try sketching much shorter lines joined together. You will find your pencil is much easier to control.

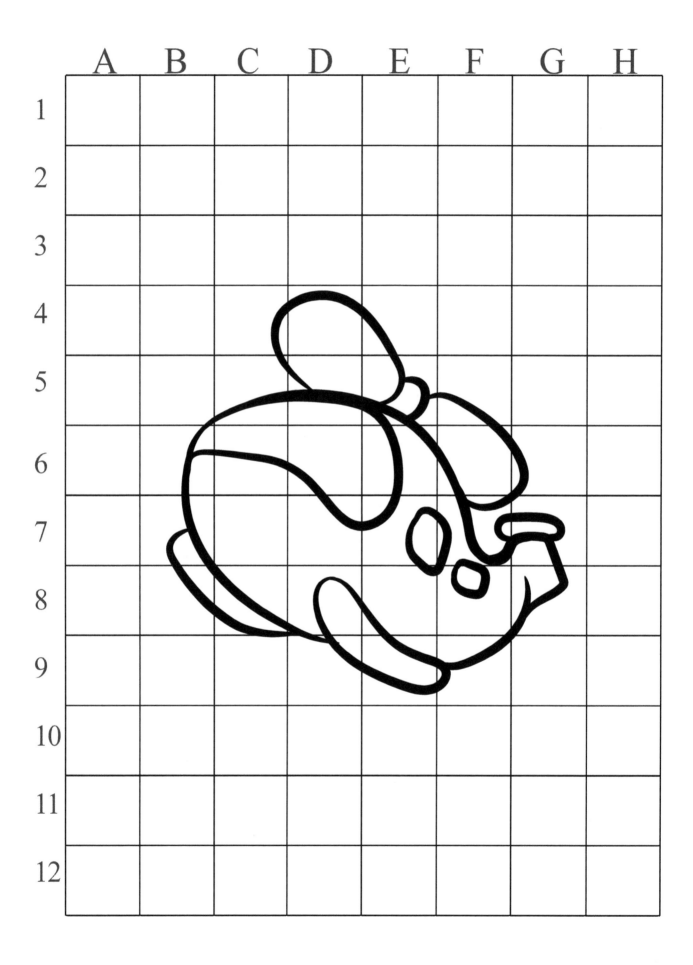

31. If you are struggling to get creative with your drawing, try listening to some music at the same time. As you concentrate on the music, your brain will still be working in the background as you draw.

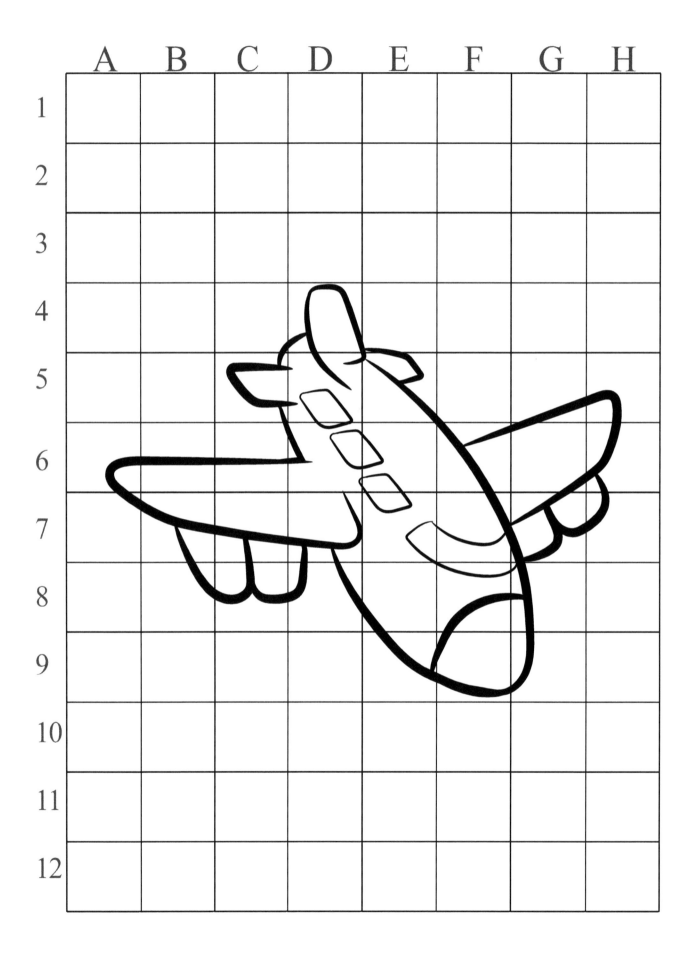

32. Much like handwriting, everyone's drawing technique is unique, so don't feel disheartened if you draw differently to your friends and siblings – they probably feel the same way!

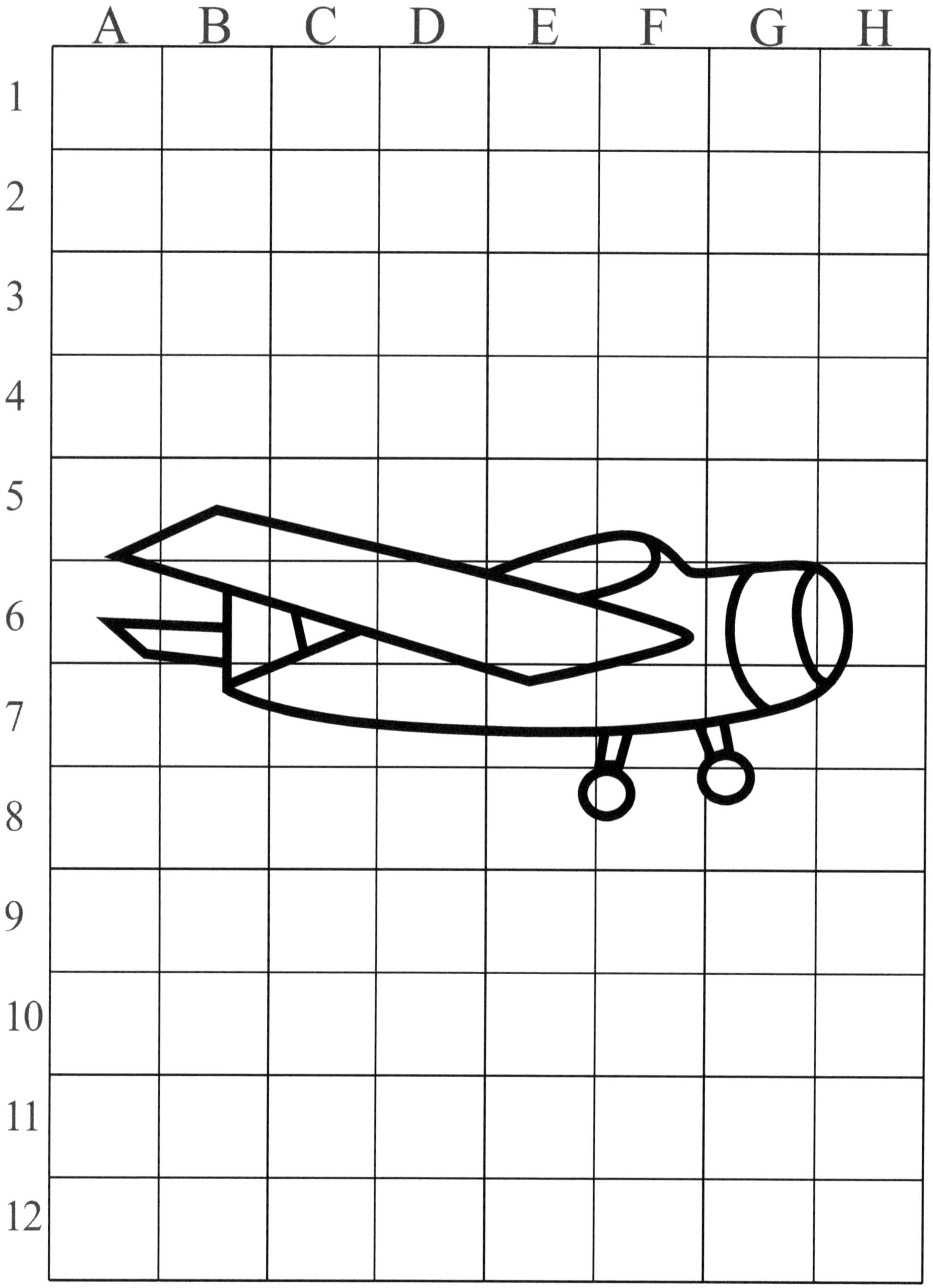
A B C D E F G H
1 2 3 4 5 6 7 8 9 10 11 12

33. Remember to take regular breaks, this will help boost your concentration and prevent you from getting too tired.

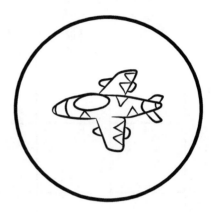

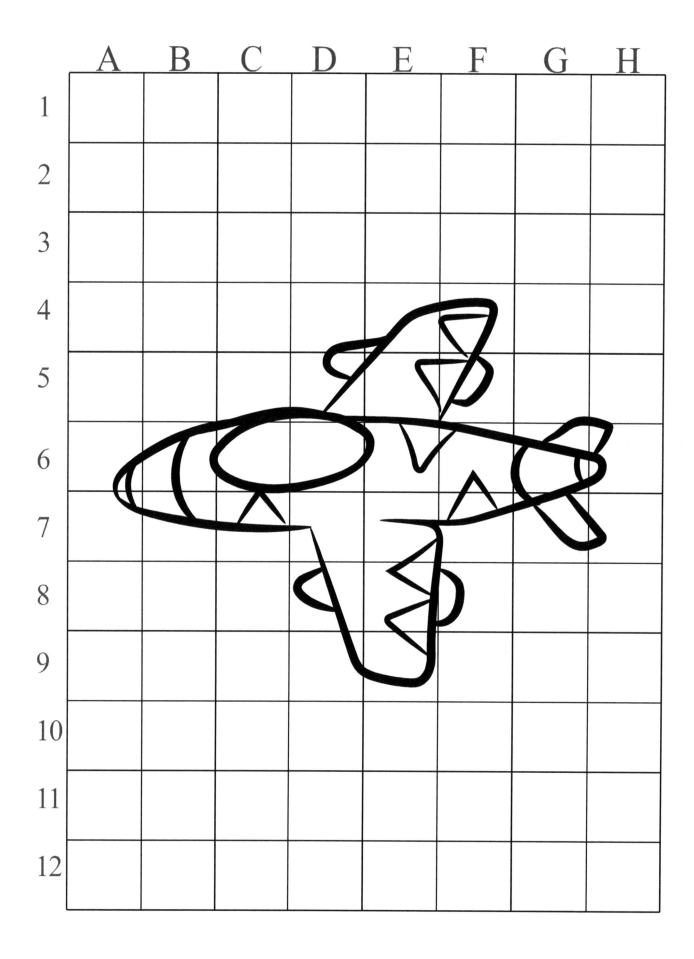

34. If you are becoming frustrated and finding the next step of the drawing a challenge, keep yourself calm and go back a few steps. By repeating the last few steps you may find this helps you flow into the step you are finding difficult.

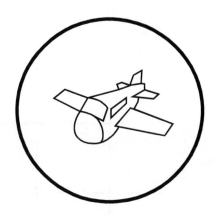

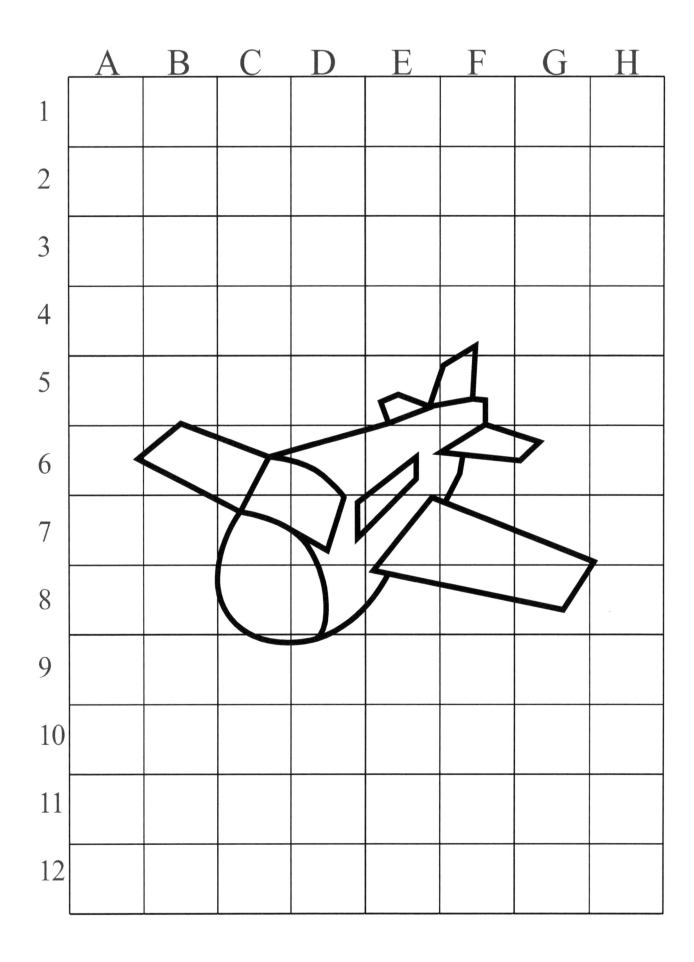

35. Everybody will make a mistake following this book, but perhaps that 'mistake' could actually become part of the drawing itself!

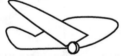

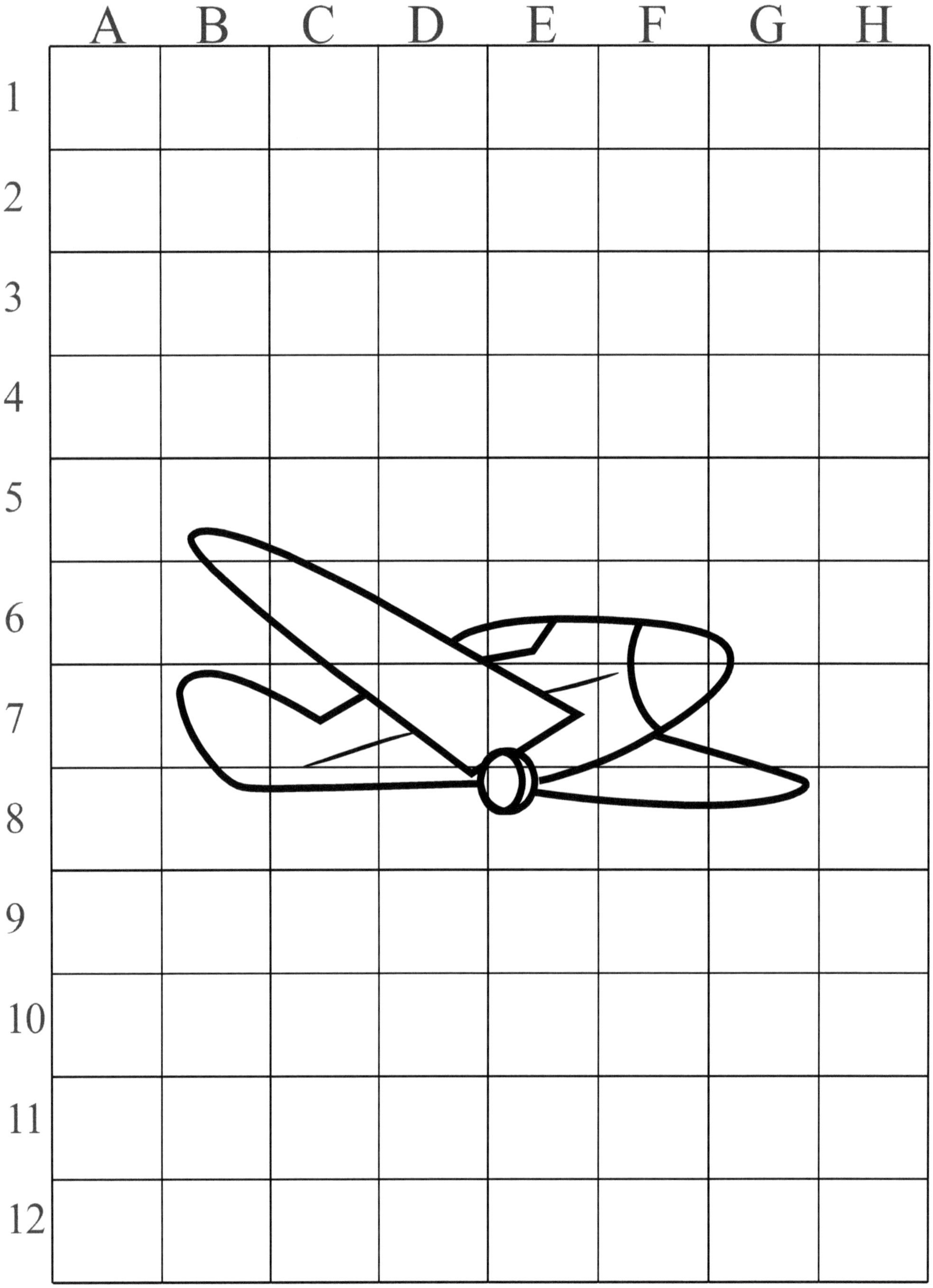

A
B
C
D
E
F
G
H
1
2
3
4
5
6
7
8
9
10
11
12

36. Anthropomorphism occurs when you give your non-human character human-like characteristics.

	A	B	C	D	E	F	G	H
1								
2								
3								
4								
5								
6								
7								
8								
9								
10								
11								
12								

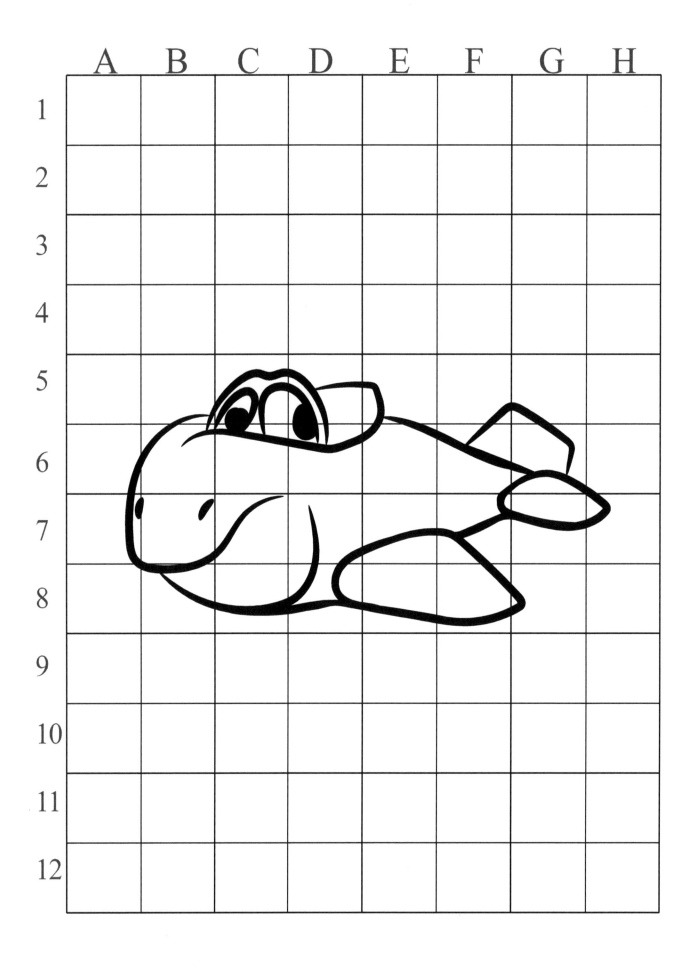

37. Here is another example of anthropomorphism.

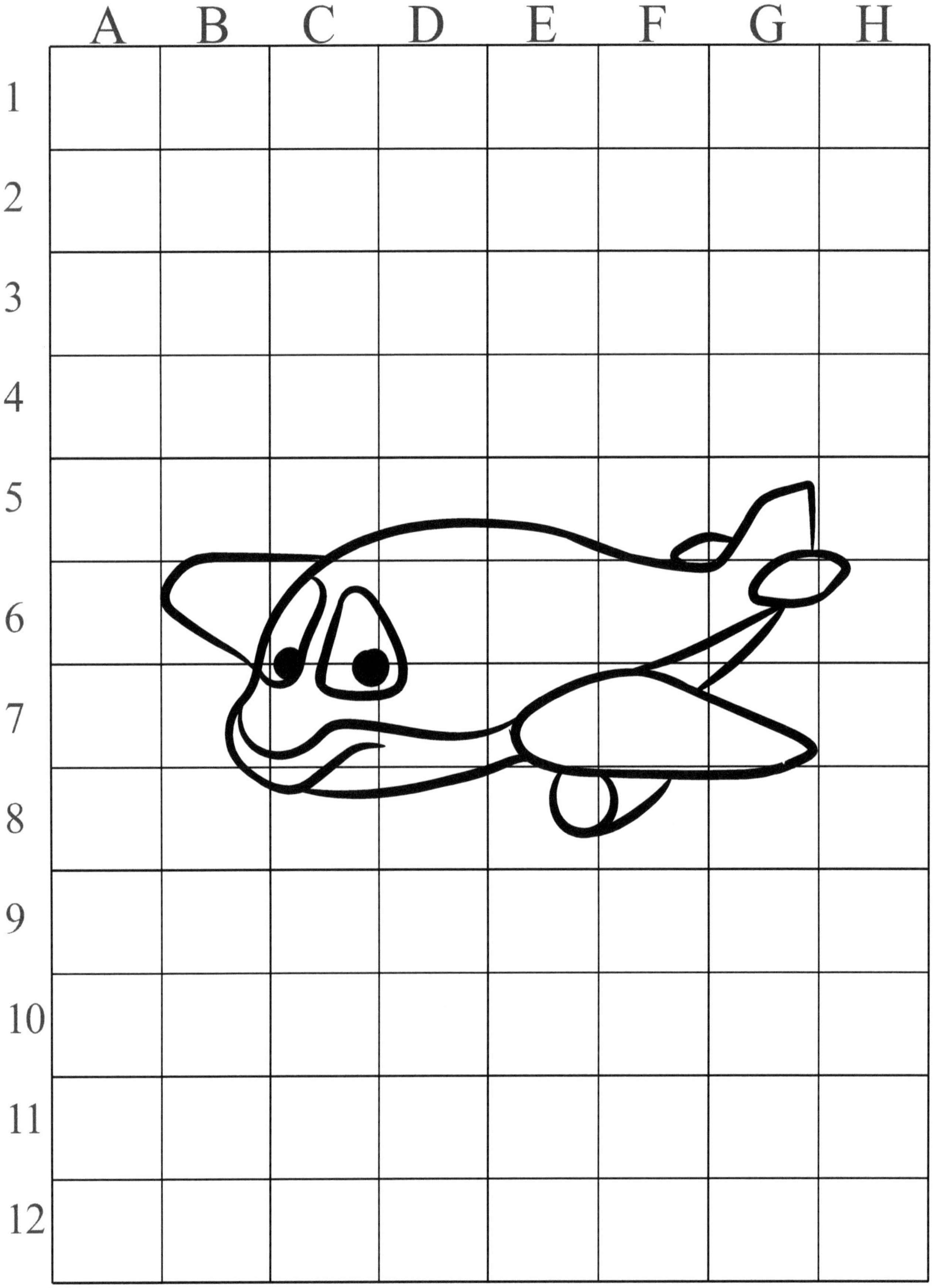
A
B
C
D
E
F
G
H
1
2
3
4
5
6
7
8
9
10
11
12

38. The angle of observation will
mean alterations in your drawing.

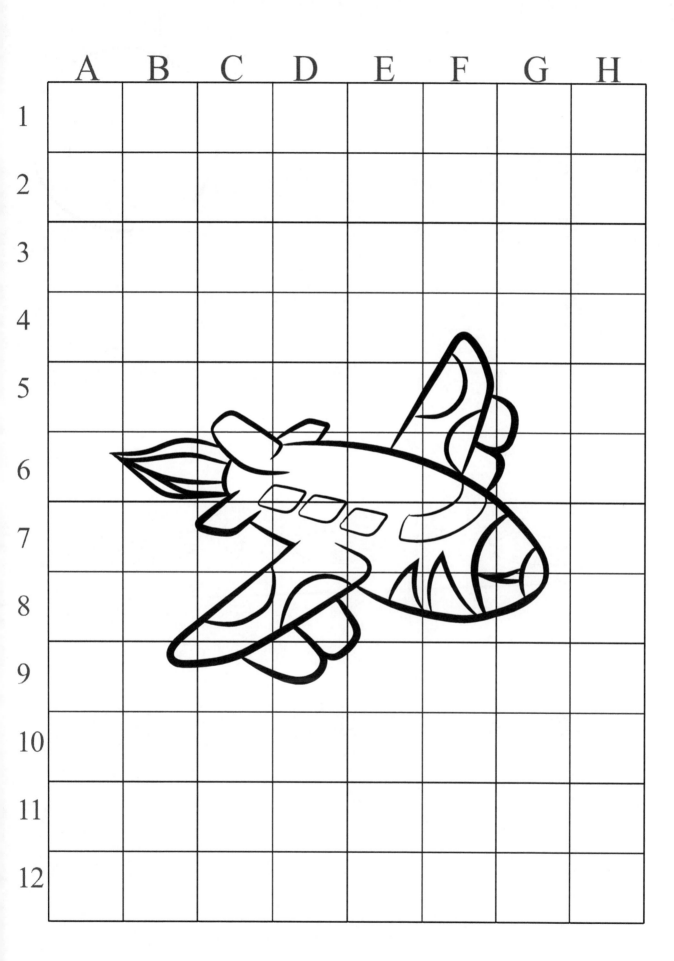

39. When you draw from a side view it is called a profile.

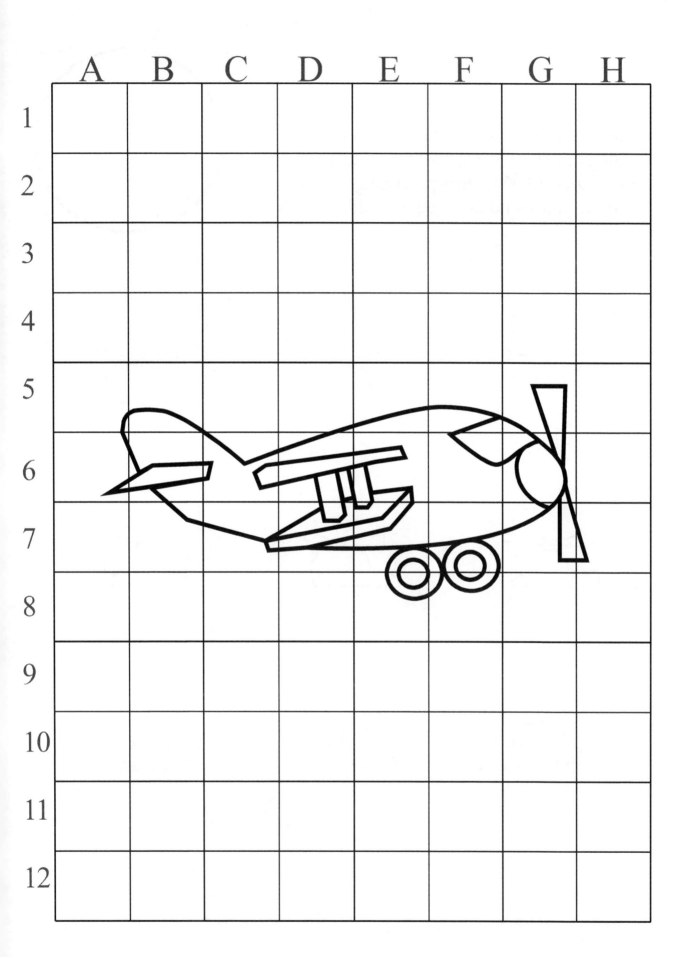

	A	B	C	D	E	F	G	H
1								
2								
3								
4								
5								
6								
7								
8								
9								
10								
11								
12								

40. To become an expert at something you may need to spend thousands of hours doing it. Expert artists will often have spent more than 10,000 hours practising. Every minute you spend drawing will add up.

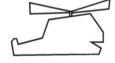

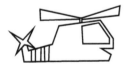

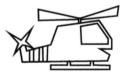

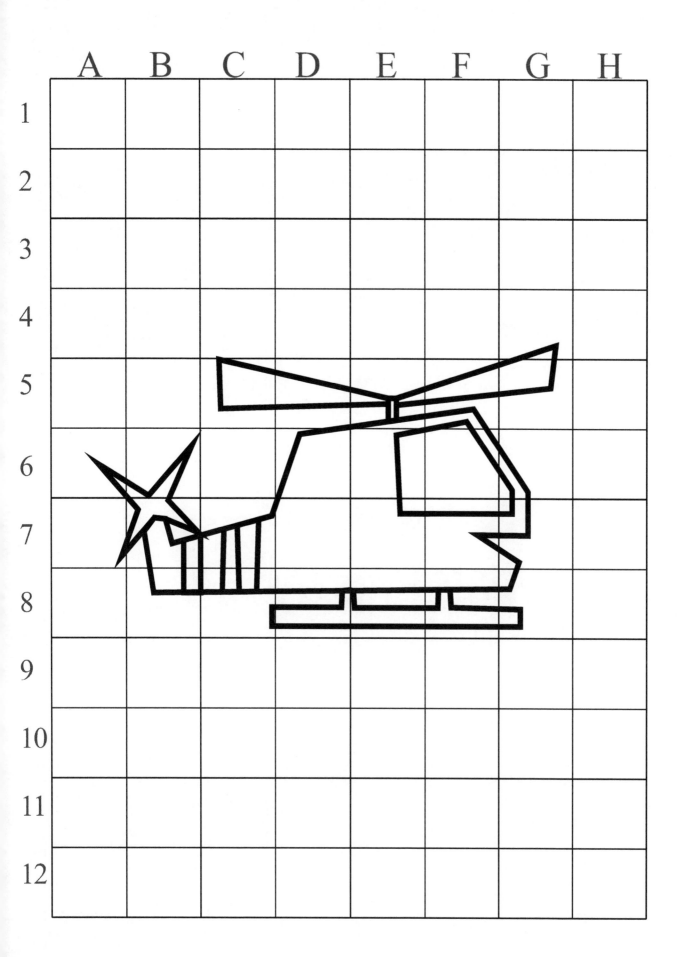

CPSIA information can be obtained
at www.ICGtesting.com
Printed in the USA
BVHW092028010222
627784BV00008B/558